the Extraordinary Journey

A SPIRITUAL ADVENTURE GUIDE
Matt Peterson

MorningStar Publications
A DIVISION OF MORNINGSTAR FELLOWSHIP CHURCH
375 Star Light Drive, Fort Mill, SC 29715
www.MorningStarMinistries.org

The Extraordinary Journey
by Matt Peterson
Copyright ©2009

Published by MorningStar Publications,
a Division of MorningStar Fellowship Church
375 Star Light Drive, Fort Mill, SC 29715
www.MorningStarMinistries.org
For information call 1-800-542-0278

International Standard Book Number: 978-1-60708-303-0; 1-60708-303-5

Unless otherwise stated, all Scripture references are taken from the New American Standard Bible. Copyright© 1960, 1962, 1963, 1968, 1971, 1973, 1974, 1977, by The Lockman Foundation. Scripture quotations marked NKJV are taken from the Holy Bible, New King James Version, © 1979, 1980, 1982 by Thomas Nelson, Inc. Scripture quotations marked KJV are taken from the King James Version of the Bible. Italics in Scripture reference for emphasis only.

No part of this book may be reproduced or transmitted in any form or by any means, electronic or mechanical, including photocopying, recording, or by any information storage or retrieval system, without permission in writing from the author.

All Rights Reserved.
Printed in the United States of America.

intro

THIS IS NOT A BOOK, it's an adventure guide. It's a practical manual to be used repeatedly—written in, carried around, worn out, coffee-stained, and torn. This book is meant to assist you as you jump into an otherworldly experience with the Lover of your soul who has already opened all of the doors and invited you through them.

The Deliberate Leap

Christianity as we have known it is due a divorce—from boredom. God never intended believers to become libraries of Christian information separate from power, adventure, and romance. Rather, we have been taken out of a dysfunctional family within the kingdom of darkness and transferred into a loving and dynamic kingdom family—a family with new, supernatural privileges.

> **For the kingdom of God does not consist in words but in power (I Corinthians 4:20).**

Every believer has been invited to live an extraordinary life of exploits and adventure. Jesus not only made the way possible for you and I to live in the impossible realm just as He lived, but He had the audacity to invite people like us to do even *greater* than what He did.

> **"Truly, truly, I say to you, he who believes in Me, the works that I do, he will do also; and greater works than these he will do; because I go to the Father" (John 14:12).**

The life of the ordinary person, faults and all, who has God living inside means that a trail of supernatural stories should be following in that person's wake—stories of exploits and lives changed forever. Jesus and the indwelling person of the Holy Spirit have overridden our shortcomings. We are new creatures now—loved creatures with new hearts and new DNA.

We were created for fellowship with the infinite God who spoke distant stars into existence. An experiential relationship with that kind of Being means that we get to see and experience what He experiences, beholding what He opens our eyes to see. Life with God is meant to be mind-blowing and heart-expanding. Devotional living with the Creator of light, sound, emotion, and vision is incapable of boredom unless we are devoted to a structure and a caricature, not a living person.

In addition to God moving from heaven to the inside of our hearts, we were created to be the conduits of heaven on the earth. The church is called to be a life-giving dispenser of truth, evicting the powers of darkness and releasing innumerable prisoners from shame. Christianity is a thriving kingdom of power, alive with the miraculous and never boring.

The epidemic of boredom in the kingdom is coming to an end as kids transferred from another domain begin to hunger for more than they have seen and experienced. Bible knowledge alone inadequately fills a child of the supernatural King. An awakening is taking place. The restless are being stirred, becoming more interested in exploits than explanations, desiring to not only learn about God, but to dream and participate with Him in extraordinary ways.

This adventure guide is a deliberate dive into the revelation of how much you are loved, swimming into realms and waters that you may not have realized existed. It's a dive into knowing and experiencing the Creator of the universe in a personal way, partnering with Him in changing the world we find ourselves in, and learning how to live beyond ourselves.

I've often been asked, "If your God exists and is a God of love, then why all of the suffering, death, and abuse of the innocent in the world?" This is a question millions have asked. In answering, I now say: First, God isn't *a* God of love. He IS LOVE. Every part of Him is love and every thought of you in His mind is initiated by love. Love and God are inseparable, indistinct, and all love flows from Him. So death and disease in the world have nothing to do with a lack of love on God's part. In fact, death and disease on the earth have more to do with a very real enemy whose job description is to "kill, steal, and destroy" (see John 10:10), and our unawareness of who we really are.

If the millions of believers were living as royalty, wielding the power of love and creativity that we have been given, the world would be filled with light and life. This leads to the second part of the answer to the question: Psalm 115:16 says: **"The heavens are the heavens of the Lord, but the earth *He has given* to the sons of men."** This verse sheds light on who is responsible for what is happening in the earth. What happens here on the earth is man's responsibility, not God's, because the earth has been given as a gift to us.

With only a small utterance, God could change the world instantly and it would be perfect, just like heaven is perfect. But He has chosen not to do so. Instead, He has chosen a bold, risky path—the path of placing those whom He made in His own image to be in charge of the planet He gave them. Our incredibly generous Parent has given us the entire earth!

The reality of what has taken place and who we are is the following: Imperfect children for whom God's Son cleansed and set free from bondage through His life, death, and resurrection are living on the planet that He created. These children, mostly unaware, have become the new home address for the most powerful spiritual force in the entire universe—the Holy Spirit. These children have become saturated with the same Spirit that raised Jesus from the dead. Not only have these loved children been forgiven and emancipated, they have also been released to enjoy God while partnering with Him in bringing His kingdom to the earth. The kingdom they get to bring includes healing people, telling stories of God's greatness, encouraging everything that breathes, and introducing people from every tribe and tongue to the Lover of their souls.

The calling from God to those He formed from dust has never been rescinded, even in the light of

Adam's sin. The Lord has given us the earth and if things are out of whack, it doesn't mean God fell asleep at the wheel. It means we get to arise and take hold of the wheel already placed in our hands, becoming what He intended us to be—sons and daughters who bring love, create ways to help people, bring light to chaos and confusion, and go to the far reaches of the planet declaring freedom to every person in His name.

Whenever I do a project around the house, my young boys beg me to let them get their hands on the tools so they can "help." They want to use a drill, hammer, saw, and screwdriver. They are not satisfied to watch their old man do all of the work. That's because it is in their DNA to *do* things, not just pray that I would do things for them, or watch me do all the work, or hope that I do all of the work. *It's in their DNA to participate.* It is in their DNA to get their hands on the tools and use them, to build something, tear something down, or fix something.

What would take me a few minutes to do around the house takes my children hours longer to accomplish. If you think we have it bad as parents, how about the eternal Father of all? He has been waiting patiently for six thousand years for His kids to use the tools and behave as His sons. The world is crying out for this. We keep waiting for Him to do it, and He patiently waits for us to pick up the power tools (gifts) He has given to us and begin the work on the world we have been given by believing that we are who He says we are. Naming the animals was just the beginning of what man was called to do here; releasing life in every sector of society has yet to happen.

The same participatory desire that my children have to build, create, and help is in our spiritual DNA from our heavenly Father—to take dominion, restore, redeem, help, heal, and release life, just like He does. You and I are sons and daughters created in His likeness, not slaves or employees. We have been placed here as His personal ambassadors to change the world He has given to us. As sons and daughters of the King of the universe, we have been born for this moment in history, for this purpose—to arise as the children of justice and release love and hope into the earth, displacing the darkness. The tools or gifts of the Spirit weren't given for us to compare our differences with others, but meant for us to enjoy as we use them to touch and change the lives of others.

The magnificent mission of Jesus was successful and complete, or **"finished" (see John 19:30)** as He Himself said. Now it's our turn to partner with Him and be light, changing the darkness. It's not God's job or the government's job to be light in the earth—it's ours. He has called us the light of the world (see Matthew 5), the salt of the earth, the ambassadors of heaven (see II Corinthians 5:20). If there is evil and abuse of the innocent, it is on our watch. It's our opportunity to arise, awake, shine, demonstrate justice, and bring the kingdom of heaven to the darkest places.

When Jesus called His disciples, He gave a brief invitation to them and was stingy with details regarding what awaited them. He then turned and started walking away—no further information, no health care benefits, no promise of safety, and no details or formulas of exactly how they should behave or pray. This method of employing world changers is disturbing to the Western mind—not enough information. After the brief invitation, it was up to the future apostles to pursue Him into the unknown, beyond the safety of details and the limitations of experience. The same invitation has been issued to every believer who has heard His voice call to them. The invitation is to **"come, follow Me" (see Mark 10:21),** beyond the comfort of the crowds and the traditions of men, into the adventures of the unknown.

> **"If anyone wishes to come after Me, he must deny himself, and take up his cross daily and follow Me" (Luke 9:23).**

Following Jesus is a life-altering opportunity to live supernaturally with Him personally, joining Him in His missions, shedding our old mindsets and perspectives, and stepping out of our spheres of comfort. If we take up the invitation, boredom and confusion will be the first things to leave. They will be replaced by an adrenaline rush of hope, peace, joy about life, thankfulness for being alive, love for others, and a brand new awareness of the remarkable God living inside of us. There will also be an increase in the sense of fulfilling the very purpose that we have been placed on the earth to fulfill.

The Extraordinary Journey began as an idea to help the people in the church I lead to become better "fit" spiritually by providing some new ways to engage God in our personal devotions as well as practical ways to touch the world. As we did this together, children included, I was surprised to find a unity we have never had as a church, a renewed excitement about the kingdom, and heights in worship we had never experienced previously. Several people told me how their personal relationships with the Lord went to brand new places, renewing their intimacy with God. We also observed some of our children stepping out in faith, becoming more courageous than the adults and excited about being used by God.

My hope is that this guide will be a springboard into new adventures and uncharted journeys with God that will change your life and the lives of many others around you. <u>Please don't view the following pages as checklists or a compulsory burden</u>, but rather <u>on-ramps into experiences and jumping points into new discoveries.</u>

I encourage you to partner up with a buddy, like a work-out partner, or do this together as a church, home group, or youth group. Your faith and spiritual muscles will be stretched in new ways. I also encourage you to go to TheXJourney.com blog and see what others are doing and experiencing.

HAVE FUN!

Jumping In

Just before diving into new waters, a certain sense of caution always precedes leaving your feet and the

the Extraordinary Journey

safety of the shore. "Am I sure I want to do this? How cold is the water going to be?"

Prior to diving into the following pages, let me mention that the water is refreshing, but you won't be fine. His waters always change us, and we never exit the water the same way we entered. His waters will whet our appetite— swimming always increases hunger.

<u>Following the journey in this book will stretch you both physically and spiritually and will certainly offend selfishness and fears that attempt to silence and render you unfruitful.</u>

As you embark on this journey, I encourage you to look at the day ahead before you get there, and plan to make time for each portion as needed, adjusting your schedule and daily plan. Perhaps some days you will not be able to complete everything, which is fine. This is meant to facilitate intimacy with the Lord and challenge you, but it is not intended to bring condemnation. Stretch yourself, but not out of religious duty. Push beyond what you think your limits are in faith but not out of compulsion.

During the "Action" portions in this guide, faith will be required. You may feel scared or fearful, particularly if trying some of these things for the first time. When given an opportunity to step out, you may feel like the hordes of hell are suddenly after you to stop and abandon course. This is just simply the resistance that comes at you from the enemy in an attempt to keep you from stepping into the supernatural. No worries, you are in good company. These are normal feelings the

the Extraordinary Journey

enemy sends to our carnal nature, <u>attempting to keep you from living the extraordinary</u>.

I have never met anyone who stepped out in faith that did not feel inadequate, unsure, or quite scared at times. The point of the action is to push beyond these fears and resistance and overcome them, learning how to live a new way. <u>Once you step out, your faith muscle will begin to grow, and you will look forward to new challenges.</u>

At the back of this guide is a section titled, "Launch Points," which is a reference section intended to help explain more about each of the launch points that you will find throughout the guide. I recommend using them often, as they will help provide a grid for engaging God in some new ways.

Included in each day's guide are blank pages for you to capture the things God speaks to you, thoughts and feelings that emerge, and highlights of your journey. I encourage you to also capture the experiences you have and the dreams you dream during the next three weeks.

The blog site, TheXJourney.com, is an important tool that works in tandem with this guide. At the blog site, numerous videos, resources, and suggested music are available to help support your journey.

There are many ways to use this guide. Some may want to use it as an intense 22-day challenge and journey. Others may want to dive into the guide once per week for 22 weeks or a mix of anything in-between. It's up to you.

the Extraordinary Journey

Equipment required

- **Books:** reading that will help you complete this journey:

    1) Bible—in a translation you enjoy

    2) *You May All Prophesy* by Steve Thompson (this will help you identify different ways that the Lord is already speaking to you). See TheXJourney.com for ordering information.

- **Computer and Internet access**

Heads Up

A one-day fast will begin this evening at 6 p.m. (after dinner) and will last until 6 p.m. the following day. No problem—you'll be sleeping for eight hours of this fast and enjoying the remaining sixteen.

It will take approximately 1 to 1.5 hours to engage in everything per day this week.

Suggestions:

- Set your alarm one hour earlier than you normally do and dive into God on Day 1.
- If you don't want to use the provided pages in this guide to journal your experiences, use a separate journal to write in.
- Begin reading *You May All Prophesy* by Steve Thompson immediately. You will need to be aware of how God is speaking to you and how to communicate to others for some of the actions included in this guide.
- Ask the Lord to speak to you in numerous ways over the next 22 days. He will.

the Extraordinary Journey

- ⊃ If you are doing this as a group or church, plan to meet around Day 11 and Day 22 to share with one another, encourage each other, and celebrate all God is doing in and through you.

- ⊃ If you are unable to complete everything each day, no problem. Either skip what you can't do or roll it over until the next day.

DAY 01

GET INTO THE HABIT *of saying "speak Lord," and life will become a romance.*

~Oswald Chambers

Receive: see Launch Point, pg. 150

BEFORE DOING ANYTHING ELSE in the day (no praying or reading yet), come before the Lord and *receive* His love. Imagine yourself in a bath of His love. Surround and soak His love into your skin for several minutes. Recognize by faith that you are already loved, accepted, pleasing to Him, and seated with Him in heavenly places. He is pleased with you before you "do" anything of merit. Read the following verses (in various translations) out loud and receive them personally. Abide in the love of Jesus and your Father. Imagine the Father and the Son looking at you, enjoying and loving you.

Read

Psalm 149:4; Jeremiah 31:3; John 3:16; Romans 8:37-39; and Romans 5:5.

Commune: see Launch Point, pg. 154

With juice or wine (if in the U.S., must be twenty-one or older), and bread (or crackers), commune with Jesus and remember Him. Read the following verses as you partake: John 6:26-64 and I Corinthians 11:23-26.

Discover: see Launch Point, pg. 160

1) Discover your birthday Scripture. For example, if your birthday is November 13, go through the Bible and look at chapters 11, verse 13 (11:13) in numerous Books and see which one God speaks to you through. If you don't find an encouraging Scripture, search your spiritual birth date instead.

2) Discover a piece of history. Google the name, William Wilberforce, and spend several minutes learning about his life. Discover the sacrifices and faith required for him to impact and change the world.

Thank: see Launch Point, pg. 155

Spend five minutes or so thanking God—not asking, just thanking Him for breath, life, Jesus, friendships, loved ones, things He has done for you in the past, salvation, the Bible, the Holy Spirit residing inside of you, love, laughter, and so on (see I Thessalonians 5:18).

Read: see Launch Point, pg. 161

Read and ingest with your spirit (see Jeremiah 15:16), not only your mind, the selected chapters: Luke 1 and 2.

Capture

Journal the things you heard, saw, felt, received, and experienced while you were doing the above. Write down your new "birthday Scripture" and what the Lord showed you through it.

Fast: see Launch Point, pg. 162

Beginning at 6 p.m. this evening, fast from all food (but drink lots of water) for one day only. Scriptural days are from "dusk to dusk."

Ask

Ask the Lord for dreams from heaven before you go to sleep tonight.

Heads Up

Fasting ends tomorrow evening at 6 p.m.

You get to impact and change someone's life tomorrow by giving something away.

Extraordinary Journal

Journal Extraordinary

Extraordinary Journal

DAY 02

*AS A SON OR A DAUGHTER of God, we have unlimited access to healing resources, love, and encouragement to give away. Anything God has given to us, we have been authorized to give away to others. **"Freely you have received, freely give" (see Matthew 10:8 NKJV).***

Note: Good morning. The plan is to repeat the "receiving" part of Day 1, both today and several other times this week. The practice of receiving and learning to receive from heaven before "doing anything" could be the most important part of this journey.

Receive

Before doing anything else in the day (no praying or reading yet), come before the Lord and *receive* His love. Imagine yourself in a bath of His love surrounding you for several minutes. Recognize by faith that you are already loved, accepted, pleasing to Him, and seated with Him in heavenly places. He is pleased with you before you "do" anything of merit. Read the following verses out loud and receive them personally. Abide in the love of Jesus and your Father. Imagine the Father and the Son looking at you, smiling and loving you.

Read

Psalms 149:4; Jeremiah 31:3; John 3:16; Romans 8:37-39; and Romans 5:5

Worship

In your native tongue, worship the Lord for a few minutes with your voice aloud. Feel free to play music to help crank it up. (See TheXJourney.com for music suggestions.)

Pray: see Launch Point, pgs. 156 and 165

Pray/speak/sing in the Spirit for ten minutes or so continuously. Allow your spirit to pray in different ways, from warlike type of tongues to worshipful melodies. Push through when you feel like stopping. Notice how your "tongue" changes as the Holy Spirit leads you in various directions.

But you, beloved, building yourselves up on your most holy faith, praying in the Holy Spirit (Jude 20).

Discover

1) Discover a birthday Scripture for a family member or friend and send it to them to encourage them.

2) Discover a piece of history. Google the name, George Muller, and spend several minutes learning about his life. Discover the sacrifices and faith required for him to impact and change the world.

Read

Taste and ingest with your spirit (see Jeremiah 15:16), not only your mind, these selected chapters: Matthew 4 and 5.

Faith in Action: see Launch Point, pg. 163

Build spiritual muscles of faith by stepping out of yourself and give away what He has already placed inside of you.

Today

With your buddy, go up to a random person that you don't know and give him or her some money (the amount is up to you). When this person asks you why you are doing this, use it as an opportunity to share how much you have been given, how lavish God is, and how you want to share it.

Capture

Capture on paper here or separately the things that you heard, saw, felt, received, and experienced while you were doing all of the above.

Fast

End your one-day fast at 6 p.m.

Enjoy

Dinner

Extraordinary Journal

Journal Extraordinary

Extraordinary Journal

DAY 03

BECOME A CONSUMMATE EXCHANGER— *adept at taking Jesus up on His standing offer to trade in all weary and heavy feelings for His light ease and restful peace (see Matthew 11:28-30).*

Exchange: see Launch Point, pg. 152

Sometimes we may wake up not "feeling" like we are Christians anymore. We may feel more like sinners than saints, feel more weight than freedom, and feel more aware of our own inadequacies than our sonship. It's time to make an exchange. Jesus is looking to trade. He's interested in every one of His loved ones coming to Him with any and every grimy, pitiful dark thought and feeling, so He can reach into the treasure chest of Himself and give us all that we need at any time, any place, and always without cost.

Wait/Listen

Wait on God without praying or straying for ten minutes. Just listen, engage your imagination in Him, quiet your soul, and fly with Him. What do you hear?

Be still, (cease striving NASB) and know that I am God (see Psalm 46:10 NKJV).

Discover

1) Discover something new about the universe God has made. Go to TheXJourney.com and look through the lenses of the Hubble telescope to see a portion of God's creation light years away.

2) Discover a piece of history. Google the name, Harriet Tubman, and spend several minutes learning about her life. In particular, look and discover the courage required for her to impact and change the world. Pay attention to what the Lord is speaking to you personally about her life.

Read

Read and ingest with your spirit (see Jeremiah 15:16), not only your mind, these selected chapters: Matthew 6 and 7.

Capture

Journal the things that you heard, saw, felt, received, and experienced while you were doing all of the above.

Laugh

Go to TheXJourney.com and click on the comedy relief videos.

Exercise: see Launch Point, pg. 166

Take several minutes and make a plan for exercising physically. Set a date to begin (*Day 5 would be a good one*). Set your own obtainable goals for losing weight, adjusting your diet, and physical exercise. Write them down. Begin exercising today for at least thirty minutes. Run/walk a mile, begin lifting weights, or do aerobics. Challenge yourself physically in ways you don't normally do.

Extraordinary Journal

DAY 04

GOD SPOKE EVERYTHING that has been created into existence, except you. You are different. In making you He came very close, intricately forming you with His own hands, tenderly designing you to love and be loved. Since that day, His thoughts have been upon you—thoughts that outnumber the grains of sand in the earth, longing for you to receive all that He has for you (see Psalm 139: 13-14).

Receive/Be Filled with the Spirit: see Launch Point, pg. 157

Come before the Lord and receive God's love and a new in-filling of His Spirit. Read Ephesians 5:18 and Acts 13:52. Picture yourself at the bottom of a waterfall and open up your mouth and your spirit. Allow the Holy Spirit to fill you to overflowing.

Discover

1) Using your street address (e.g., "198"), look up variations of this number in the Bible and see what God shows you regarding where you live. As an example, look up *Strong's* number 198 (insert your address number), or chapter 19, verse 8. Or, read the passage on page "198" in your Bible and see what the Lord may show you.

2) Discover a piece of history. Google the name, Ludwig Von Zinzendorf.

Read

Read and ingest in your spirit (see Jeremiah 15:16), not only your mind, these selected chapters. Luke 9 and 10. *While reading, notice how Jesus sends people out to minister before they are "qualified."*

Capture

Journal the things that you heard, saw, felt, received, and experienced while you were doing all of the above.

Serve: see Launch Point, pg. 167

Give ten minutes of your time and service to someone, helping them in some way (washing dishes, a massage for your spouse, cleaning someone's car, run errands for someone, help your neighbor, etc.). Ask someone what you can do to help them, and then do it.

Faith in Action

Find something in your home, office, or attic to give away to someone—something nice and something of value. Ask the Lord to show you someone to give it to and what to give, then set the giving process in motion.

Rest

Spend at least one hour doing something restful and enjoyable. Take a nap, read a book, or watch a movie.

Journal Extraordinary

Extraordinary Journal

DAY 05

MEN FAIL, GOVERNMENTS FAIL, *ministries fail, our best efforts sometimes fail—but love never will. Love is an unfailing power, a transforming force. Those who learn to wield and dispense this weapon will change the course of history, populating the ranks of heaven.*

Watch

See what love can do. Go to TheXJourney.com and view the love video.

Receive

Before doing anything else in the day, come before the Lord and receive His love. Bathe in His love for several minutes. Recognize by faith that you are already loved, accepted, pleasing to Him, and seated with Him in heavenly places. Read Psalm 149:4; Jeremiah 31:3; John 3:16; Romans 8:37-39; and Romans 5:5.

Commune

With juice or wine (if in the U.S., must be twenty-one or older), and bread (or crackers), commune with Jesus and remember Him. Read the following Scriptures as you partake: John 6:26-64 and I Corinthians 11:23-26.

Thank

Spend five minutes or so thanking God for things you have never thanked Him for. Get creative and look around. Have you ever thanked Him for indoor plumbing, hot water, your refrigerator, Moses, Enoch, or for a beating heart and expanding lungs? The world is full of the lavishness of God.

Discover

1) License Plate. Look at the license plate letters and numbers on your vehicle. Ask God to show you what (if anything) this speaks of. Possibly look up the numbers as chapters and verses in the Bible and see what He may show you personally. Maybe Google them or see what the corresponding *Strong's Concordance* number relates to. If you have more than one vehicle, look up those letters/numbers also. Vehicles often speak of our personal ministry. I wouldn't be surprised that while you are searching this, God shows you something related to your calling in ministry.

2) Discover a piece of history. Google the name, John G. Lake, and spend several minutes learning about his life. Discover the incredible faith and powerful healings that John participated in.

Read

Before reading today's chapters (see Luke 11 and 12), ask the Holy Spirit to bring revelation to your heart and mind as you read, and then get ready for insight that will amaze you. Also, read these in other translations than you typically use. Try the *Wuest* or *The Message*.

Faith in Action

Confront a fear by talking to someone you don't know. Give him or her a drink of the living waters already inside of you.

With your buddy, go up to someone in public that you do not know and give them an encouraging word (for a prophetic word—refer to what you are learning in *You May All Prophesy* and see I Corinthians 14:3). This can be very simple, not long. Prophecy is primarily encouragement. Ask God about a particular person and find something good and encouraging to say to them. Celebrate their heroic journey. Stay away from negative, condescending words.

Capture

Journal the things that you heard, saw, felt, received, and experienced while you were doing all of the above.

Exercise

Begin your exercise plan today. Run/walk a mile, begin lifting weights, or do aerobics. Change your eating habits and challenge yourself physically in ways you don't normally do.

Extraordinary Journal

Journal Extraordinary

Extraordinary Journal

YOU ARE A MYSTERY SPEAKER, *a communicator of the hidden treasures of the kingdom in a language that the enemy does not understand. With confidence and frequency, release heaven's syllables into earth's atmosphere and into your private world.*

For one who speaks in a tongue does not speak to men but to God; for no one understands, but in his spirit he speaks mysteries (see I Corinthians 14:2).

Exchange

Your freedom is a breath away; it's already yours. Your effort is to believe, not "do." Jesus is looking to trade this morning. Give Him every care and concern—everything you don't like about yourself for everything you love about Him. His transformation comes through exchanging your everything for His. Take a few minutes and exchange with Him by faith; trade way up.

Receive/Be Filled with the Spirit

Come before the Lord and imagine yourself at the bottom of a waterfall. Open up your mouth and your spirit. Allow the Holy Spirit to fill you to overflowing. Do this for several minutes. Read Ephesians 5:18 and John 3:34.

Worship

In your native tongue, worship the Lord for a few minutes with your voice. Feel free to play music to help.

Pray

Pray/speak/sing in the Spirit for ten minutes (or so) continuously today. Allow your spirit to pray in different ways, from warlike tongues to worshipful melodies. Notice how your tongue changes as the Holy Spirit leads you in different ways.

But you, beloved, building yourselves up on your most holy faith, praying in the Holy Spirit (Jude 20).

Discover

1) Discover the Lord's heart toward you. Ask the Lord what He is thinking about you right now. Listen for His answer and write down what you hear.

2) Discover a piece of history. Google the name, Fanny Crosby, and spend several minutes learning about her life. Look and discover the sacrifices and faith required for this person to impact and change the world.

Read

Again, begin by asking the Holy Spirit to reveal Himself to you as you read. Read and ingest with your spirit, not only your mind, the following selected chapters: John 14 and 15. These are two of the most powerful chapters in all of the Bible.

Break a Cycle: see Launch Point pg. 169

Fast from *all* criticism and negative thinking about others. Also fast from negative words and thoughts about yourself today (see Ephesians 4:29; Romans 2:1; Matthew 7:1).

Turn Around

Acknowledge all criticism and judgment ever thought and spoken out about your parents, people you work with, your pastor, people in your church, and government leaders. Ask Jesus to forgive you and break off any and all of those words toward them and the boomerang result toward yourself. Begin saying out loud the names of those you have criticized in the past and now begin blessing them with hope and gracious words, asking God to do great things for them.

Faith in Action

Say out loud to yourself "I am the light of world" (see Matthew 5:14) and "God's kingdom lives inside of me" (see Luke 17:21). You are about to give someone a drink of the living waters already inside of you.

Action Today

With your buddy, go to a grocery store today and find someone that you do not know who is wearing a blue shirt. Go up to that person and give an encouraging prophetic word (see I Corinthians 14:3).

Keep it encouraging and it will have power. This is love reaching its destination.

Capture

Journal the things that you heard, saw, felt, received, and experienced while you were doing all of the above.

Blog

Blog the experiences you want to share at TheXJourney.com.

Journal Extraordinary

Extraordinary Journal

DAY 07

THE HEART OF THE AWAKENED *believer looks expectantly among the commonplace activities of life for opportunities to let God's love leak out of them.*

Note: As you begin your seventh day, I encourage you to start this morning in a warm bathtub or quiet/comfortable place where you don't normally go.

Receive

Rest in Him before doing anything. Read, say these verses out loud, and receive them personally. Abide in the love of Jesus and your Father. Imagine Them loving you. Read Psalm 149:4; Jeremiah 31:3; John 3:16; and Romans 8:37-39.

Wait/Listen

Wait on God without praying or straying for ten minutes. Just listen, engage your imagination in Him, and fly with Him.

> **Be still, (cease striving NASB) and know that I am God (see Psalm 46:10 NKJV).**

Thank

Spend five minutes or so thanking God. Create your own "thank you song" to the Lord today, thanking

Him for the small and the great. Thank Him for breath, life, Jesus, friendships, and things He has done for you in the past. Thank Him for the Bible and all that has gone into preserving it for you, for the Holy Spirit residing inside of you, for love, for laughter, for the USA, etc. Read I Thessalonians 5:18.

Dress Up

Put on all of the armor described in Ephesians 6:13-17. Read it and by faith through action, put on each one for all that is ahead today.

Discover

Discover a piece of history. Google the name, Frederick Douglass, and spend several minutes learning about his life. Discover the sacrifices and faith required for this person to impact and change the world.

Read

Sometime before going to sleep tonight, read and ingest John 16 and Mark 16.

Keep Breaking the Cycle

Continue fasting from *all* criticism and negative thinking about anyone including yourself (see Ephesians 4:29).

Faith in Action

Action today: With your buddy, go to a coffee shop and find someone wearing red. Ask the Lord for an encouraging prophetic word for him or her and give it. Read I Corinthians 14:3.

Capture

Capture the things that you heard, saw, felt, received, and experienced while you were doing all of the above.

Exercise at least 30 minutes

Set your own goal and plan for exercising. Run/walk a mile, begin lifting weights, or do aerobics. Change eating habits, and challenge yourself physically in ways you don't normally do.

Fast

In preparation for week 2: Fast from all food for two days (water only)—Days 8 and 9. I recommend starting at 6 p.m. tonight (after dinner) and ending at 6 p.m. on Day 9.

Blog

Blog the experiences that you want to share at TheXJourney.com.

Extraordinary Journal

Journal Extraordinary

Extraordinary Journal

WEEK 02

Heads Up

Heading into week two, some of the actions will require greater faith.

Also, we begin week two with two days of fasting from food. As before, you will start at dusk (6 p.m.) and eat again forty-eight hours later. If you haven't already, read the "Fasting" launch point at the end of this book (see pages 162-163). It will help.

It will take approximately 1.5 to 2 hours per day to complete everything.

Suggestions:

- ➲ This week, set your alarm to get up 1.5 hours earlier than you normally would.
- ➲ Movie: Watch *The Passion of the Christ* sometime this week.

Extraordinary Journal

BELIEVING IS THE SUPERSONIC vehicle that transports us from the soup of the mundane to the banquet table of the impossible. Our job description is to believe, to become full-time believers in the face of doubt, common sense, and intellectualism. The outrageous statements of Jesus beckon us to climb aboard (see John 6:29, 14:12).

Note: Good morning. Let's start off week two and this day by walking around outside for a few minutes (or as long as you can, depending on weather). Receive God's love while walking around; bathe in Him while breathing in the brisk air. We will also begin some proclamations this week that will change the atmosphere. Have a life-changing week.

Believe: see Launch Point, pg. 168

While outside, consider the following verses and choose to believe that what He said is true. Physically jump and take a leap into believing that His Words are true.

> I am the righteousness of God in Jesus Christ (see II Corinthians 5:21).

"I am the Light of the world" (see John 8:12).

It is no longer I who live, but Christ who lives in me (see Galatians 2:20).

I have been forgiven of all my sins entirely. God remembers them no longer (see Hebrews 8:12).

I am a new creation. All of the old things have passed away (see II Corinthians 5:17).

Commune: Inside or Outside

With juice or wine (if in the U.S., must be twenty-one or older) and bread (or crackers), commune with Jesus and remember Him. Look up and read the following Scriptures as you partake: John 6:26-64 and I Corinthians 11:23-26.

Thanks

Spend five minutes or so thanking God—not asking, just thanking Him. Thank Him for friends, opportunities, finances, resources, for your vehicle, residence, for hope, forgiveness, peace, joy, and so on.

Proclaim: see Launch Point, pg. 171

Stand up (on a chair, the stairs, or on a bed if safe and possible) and proclaim out loud like you mean it, the following over your life *every day* this week (yeah, it will feel a little odd).

I am loved. I am forgiven. I know the Father of heaven and His strong Son personally. Greater is the Person inside of me than any force in the world. Jesus loves me, has set me free, and released me from all bondage. I am no longer my own, but Jesus has purchased me and I am made in His image. My mind, body, and spirit are His. I am no longer a slave to sin or fear or poverty thinking. I am not afraid any longer. I have been purchased by the living blood of Jesus and cleansed from all of my past. I have the mind of Jesus Christ.

The Holy Spirit Himself resides inside of me right now, and inside my heart is His home address. All things are becoming new in my life. I am a daughter/son of the Father of love. I have no limitations in Christ. I can do everything that Jesus did and even greater things. I have full access to the Father through Jesus, and I am seated in heaven right now with Him. I have a purpose to fulfill on this earth. Through Jesus, I have been given authority over all of the power of the enemy. I hear the voice of God, and I am an ambassador of His love to others on this earth. I am a New Covenant creature, and I will follow Jesus today into every adventure He leads me into. He has a purpose for me to fulfill. I will love the unlovable; I will see with His eyes. I will freely give away to others what He has given me. I will see the lost saved. I will see the dead raised. I will serve and obey the one I love and Who loved me first—Jesus. I am becoming His best friend.

Read

Romans 1 and 2.

Discover

Discover what it's like to walk around outside and ask God questions about His creation like Adam and

Eve did. Think about the trees, the stars, the birds, and ask Him questions about them. Imagine walking with Him in His garden and Him explaining to you why He did things the way He did.

Fast

Continue the two-day fast. Look up references to "fasting" in the Scriptures and discover why fasting is important and powerful.

Faith in Action

Build spiritual muscle through faith by doing the daily faith action.

Action today: See yourself as God's ambassador in the earth (see II Corinthians 5:20). Take a buddy (if possible), and together go up to someone in public (at a coffee shop, Wal-Mart, the mall, farmer's market, etc.) that you don't know and ask if he or she needs prayer for anything (healing, emotional, family member, problem, and so forth). Then pray for that person in faith if allowed to. Release the kingdom already in you.

Capture

Capture anything that you heard, saw, felt, or experienced from the day so far. Make sure to write down any dreams that you have had also.

Heads Up

You probably don't need a reminder that fasting ends on Day 9 at 6 p.m.

Journal Extraordinary

Extraordinary Journal

YOU ARE NOT CALLED to be a good citizen or a good child only, but rather a dispenser of heavenly potion, an authorized dealer of kindness and a lavish lover of both God and man. You are fat with His presence, robust with His wisdom, and loved before you were born. You, in your current state, are the desire of your Father and the chosen child with a unique mission to complete.

Exchange

Your freedom is a breath away. It's already yours. Our effort is to believe, not do. Jesus is looking to trade this morning. Give Him every care, concern, and everything you don't like about yourself for everything you love about Him. His transformation comes through exchanging our everything for His. Take a few minutes and exchange with Him, trade way up.

Receive/Be Filled with the Spirit

Picture yourself at the bottom of a waterfall. Open up your mouth and your spirit. Allow the Holy Spirit to fill you to overflowing. Read: Ephesians 5:18 and John 3:34.

Worship

Play your favorite song and worship along with it. Maybe replay it a couple of times too. (Suggestion: Jonathan Helser's song "Intimacy.")

Pray: See Launch Point Access, pg. 159

Pray/speak/sing in the Spirit for fifteen minutes continuously today.

While praying in the Spirit, think about the kingdom of God coming to your town, city, home, office, church, or neighborhood. Let your language follow the Spirit to release heaven toward these things (see Matthew 6:10). Pray with authority and confidence.

While praying in the Spirit, pray for those you know who are sick or have diseases that need to be healed. Pray out loud and proclaim their healing.

Proclaim

Today, go into your bathroom and stand in front of your mirror. Looking yourself in the eyes, proclaim this over yourself:

I am loved. I am forgiven. I know the Father of heaven and His strong Son personally. Greater is the Person inside of me than any force in the world. Jesus loves me, has set me free, and released me from all bondage. I am no longer my own, but Jesus has purchased me and I am made in His image. My mind, body, and spirit are His. I am no longer a slave to sin or fear or poverty thinking. I am not afraid any longer. I have been purchased by the living blood of Jesus and cleansed from all of my past. I have the mind of Jesus Christ.

The Holy Spirit Himself resides inside of me right now, and inside my heart is His home address. All things are becoming new in my life. I am a daughter/son of the Father of love. I have no limitations in Christ. I can do everything that Jesus did and even greater things. I have full access to the Father through Jesus, and I am seated in heaven right now with Him. I have a purpose to fulfill on this earth. Through Jesus, I have been given authority over all of the power of the enemy. I hear the voice of God, and I am an ambassador of His love to others on this earth. I am a New Covenant creature, and I will follow Jesus today into every adventure He leads me into. He has a purpose for me to fulfill. I will love the unlovable; I will see with His eyes. I will freely give away to others what He has given me. I will see the lost saved. I will see the dead raised. I will serve and obey the One I love and Who loved me first—Jesus. I am becoming His best friend.

Read

Romans 3 and 4.

Discover

1) Discover something about the immensity of the universe that God formed and holds together (see Hebrews 1), by going to TheXJourney.com and view universe images.

2) Discover five Scriptures about healing—one from the Psalms, three from the Book of Matthew, and one from Peter. Write them down as well as what

the Lord illuminates with each of them in your Capture. As additional study, listen to "Healing, our Neglected Birthright" teaching series by Bill Johnson (ibethel.org).

Faith in Action

Do at least one of the following today with your buddy:

1) Go up to someone at the mall, library, or other public place, and ask him or her if prayer is needed for anything (healing, emotional, a family member, problem, and so forth). Pray for that person in faith if allowed to, releasing the healing Jesus purchased for them.

2) Go to a public place and begin sharing out loud the "hope that is within you." With people around, share your testimony or the gospel message.

Capture

Capture anything that you heard, saw, felt, or experienced from the day so far. Make sure to write down any dreams that you have had also.

Fast

End your two-day fast at 6 p.m.

Enjoy

Dinner

Journal Extraordinary

Extraordinary Journal

"COME DINE WITH ME" is the open invitation from Papa to enjoy a meal and moment with Him (see Luke 22; Revelation 3:20).

Note: If possible, drive or go to a park, mountain, or outdoor place to do the following today.

Receive

Read, say these verses out loud, and receive them personally. Abide in the love of your Father. Imagine Him loving you. Read: Mark 1:11; Galatians 2:20; I John 4:9; and Romans 5:5.

Commune

With juice or wine (if twenty-one or older) and bread (or crackers), commune with Jesus and remember Him. Receive all that He has for you—all of His power and love. Exchange with Him. Read: John 6; I Corinthians 11:23-26.

Wait/Listen

Wait on God without praying or straying for ten minutes. The key is listening, focusing on Him, watching, and expecting Him to communicate with you (see Psalm 46:10).

Pray

Pray/speak/sing in the Spirit for fifteen minutes continuously today.

- Pray for the kingdom of God to come to your city, home, office, church, and neighborhood (see Matthew 6:10).
- Pray for those you know who are sick or have diseases to be healed. Speak out loud and proclaim their healing.

Proclaim

Stand up and out loud, saying it like you mean it, proclaim the following over your life *every day* this week:

I am loved. I am forgiven. I know the Father of heaven and His strong Son personally. Greater is the Person inside of me than any force in the world. Jesus loves me, has set me free, and released me from all bondage. I am no longer my own, but Jesus has purchased me and I am made in His image. My mind, body, and spirit are His. I am no longer a slave to sin or fear or poverty thinking. I am not afraid any longer. I have been purchased by the living blood of Jesus and cleansed from all of my past. I have the mind of Jesus Christ.

The Holy Spirit Himself resides inside of me right now, and inside my heart is His home address. All things are becoming new in my life. I am a daughter/son of the Father of love. I have no limitations in Christ. I can do everything that Jesus did and even greater things. I have full access to the Father through Jesus, and I am seated in heaven right now with Him. I have a purpose to fulfill on this earth. Through Jesus, I have been given authority over all of the power of the enemy. I hear the voice of God, and I am an ambassador of His love to others on this earth. I am a New Covenant creature, and I will follow Jesus today into every adventure He leads me into. He has a purpose for me to fulfill. I will love the unlovable; I will see with His eyes. I will freely give away to others what He has given me. I will see the lost saved. I will see the dead raised. I will serve and obey the One I love and Who loved me first—Jesus. I am becoming His best friend.

Read

Romans 5 and 6.

Fast

Fast from watching TV/movies/Internet for one full day (other than work related/necessary things), choosing to pursue and prefer the Lord instead. Taste and see that He is good.

Discover

1) Discover something new about your spouse and children, co-worker, or friend. Ask them questions about their stories, about their favorites, and about their dreams. Take time to discover hidden treasures in them.
2) Discover something that happened on this day in history.

Laugh

Ingest the best medicine—laughter. Look at your problems and begin laughing at them.

Go to TheXJourney.com and watch one of the laugh videos.

Faith in Action

Build spiritual muscle through faith by doing one of the following daily faith actions with your buddy.

1) Go into a business and ask the owners if they will allow you and your buddy to pray over their business and bless it. If permitted, commit their business to the Lord and release a blessing upon it.

2) Go up to someone in public that you see is physically struggling, hurt, or in need. Ask if you can pray for them and release the kingdom upon them.

Capture

Capture anything that you heard, saw, felt, or experienced from the day so far. Make sure to write down any dreams that you have had also.

Blog

Blog the experiences you want to share at TheXJourney.com.

Exercise

Exercise for at least thirty minutes today.

Journal Extraordinary

Extraordinary Journal

AS THE PATH OF LIFE *wanders through the valley, piles of bones can be seen littering either side. These dry bones belong to believers who let discouragement consume their hope; those who considered the whispers of the accuser, taking their eyes off the prize. To all who have given up hope, the same resurrection words that Lazarus heard are being spoken over you this morning: "Come forth." The tomb has released you to live again.*

Shake Off

Shake off all doubt, all insecurity, and all feelings of inadequacy. Jesus is your adequacy and He has made you adequate as His minister, as His ambassador, and as His loved one. Flush hopelessness; your Redeemer has risen with power! (see II Corinthians 3:5-6 and Romans 8:11)

Dress Up

Put on all of the armor described in Ephesians 6:13-17. Read it and put on each one for all that is ahead today.

Thanks

Spend five minutes or so thanking God—not asking, just thanking Him (thank Him for finances, resources, your vehicle, residence, for hope, forgiveness, peace, joy, and so on).

Proclaim

Go to your mirror again and look yourself in the eyes. Out loud, saying it like you mean it, proclaim this over your life today:

I am loved. I am forgiven. I know the Father of heaven and His strong Son personally. Greater is the Person inside of me than any force in the world. Jesus loves me, has set me free, and released me from all bondage. I am no longer my own, but Jesus has purchased me and I am made in His image. My mind, body, and spirit are His. I am no longer a slave to sin or fear or poverty thinking. I am not afraid any longer. I have been purchased by the living blood of Jesus and cleansed from all of my past. I have the mind of Jesus Christ.

The Holy Spirit Himself resides inside of me right now, and inside my heart is His home address. All things are becoming new in my life. I am a daughter/son of the Father of love. I have no limitations in Christ. I can do everything that Jesus did and even greater things. I have full access to the Father through Jesus, and I am seated in heaven right now with Him. I have a purpose to fulfill on this earth. Through Jesus, I have been given authority over all of the power of the enemy. I hear the voice of God, and I am an ambassador of His love to others on this earth. I am a New Covenant creature, and I will follow Jesus today into every adventure He leads me into. He has a purpose for me to fulfill. I will love the unlovable; I will see with His eyes. I will freely give away to others what He has given me. I will see the lost saved. I will see the dead raised. I will serve and obey the One I love and Who loved me first—Jesus. I am becoming His best friend.

Read

Romans 7 and 8.

Create

The most creative Person in the universe lives inside of you. Ask Him for creative ideas, then create something (write a poem or song, build a craft, draw a picture, paint a scene, capture an image of creation, and so on).

Fast

Fast from all criticism, all negative talk about anyone (including yourself), and from thinking about past things (see Ephesians 4:29, Philippians 3:10-13, and Matthew 12:36-37).

Slip Away

If at work today, take a five-minute break and slip away to an alone place and get filled back up again with His Spirit. Sit at the bottom of the waterfall of God's love. In moments, you will get filled back up. Jesus would often **"slip away" (see Luke 5:16)** to pray.

Faith in Action

Do at least one of the following today.

1) See yourself as the light of the world (see Matthew 5:14). Imagine a person in your mind that you know who lives in another state or country, and

the Extraordinary Journey

then pray and ask God for a prophetic word for them (see I Corinthians 14:3). Then e-mail them the word of encouragement that you received.

2) With your buddy, go to a public place and ask the Lord to show you a person who is in need of physical healing. Go to the first person you see who is limping, lame, blind, using a hearing aid, or in a wheelchair, and ask them if you can pray for them. Tell them that the kingdom of God is at hand (see Matthew 10:7), and then heal them.

3) Give a prophetic word to a Christian that you know who does not believe in the power of the Holy Spirit and does not believe that God still speaks. Ask God for a specific word to encourage them and give it.

Serve

Give ten minutes to someone to help them in numerous ways (washing dishes, a massage for your spouse, cleaning someone's car, run errands for someone, help your neighbor, and so on). Ask someone what you can do to serve them.

Rest

Spend one hour doing something restful. Take a nap, read a book, or play a game.

Capture

Capture anything you heard, saw, felt, or experienced from the day so far. Make sure to write down any dreams that you have also had.

Extraordinary Journal

Extraordinary Journal

DAY 12

OFTEN THERE IS A CANYON between what I hold to be true and how I live. Bridging this distance requires putting motion to what I believe, departing from the comfortable, and stepping over into difficult. Heaven touches the natural things when the carriers of heaven walk where fear tells them not to go.

New Breath

Use your imagination and picture Jesus breathing His Spirit into you this morning like a refreshing wind.

He breathed on them and said to them, "Receive the Holy Spirit" (see John 20:22).

Inhale wave after wave of the Holy Spirit. This is the Spirit given without measure.

Abide

Read John 15 and begin to learn what it means to "stay and not leave" Him.

Pray

Pray/speak/sing in the Spirit for fifteen minutes continuously today.

- Ask God for an interpretation to what you prayed in the Spirit. Write it down.
- Pray for the kingdom of God to come to the United States, your city, home, office, church, and neighborhood (see Matthew 6:10).
- Pray for those you know who are sick or have diseases to be healed. Speak out loud and proclaim their healing.

Read

Eat (see Jeremiah 15:16), ingest, and meditate on the following passages: Hebrews 1 and 2.

Proclaim

Out loud, saying it like you mean it, proclaim this over your life today:

I am loved. I am forgiven. I know the Father of heaven and His strong Son personally. Greater is the Person inside of me than any force in the world. Jesus loves me, has set me free, and released me from all bondage. I am no longer my own, but Jesus has purchased me and I am made in His image. My mind, body, and spirit are His. I am no longer a slave to sin or fear or poverty thinking. I am not afraid any longer. I have been purchased by the living blood of Jesus and cleansed from all of my past. I have the mind of Jesus Christ.

The Holy Spirit Himself resides inside of me right now, and inside my heart is His home address. All things are becoming new in my life. I am a daughter/son of the Father of love. I have no limitations in Christ. I can do everything that Jesus did and even greater things. I have full access to the Father through Jesus, and I am seated in heaven right now with Him. I have a purpose to fulfill on this earth. Through Jesus, I have been given authority over all of the power of the enemy. I hear the voice of God, and I am an ambassador of His love to others on this earth. I am a New Covenant creature, and I will follow Jesus today into every adventure He leads me into. He has a purpose for me to fulfill. I will love the unlovable; I will see with His eyes. I will freely give away to others what He has given me. I will see the lost saved. I will see the dead raised. I will serve and obey the One I love and Who loved me first—Jesus. I am becoming His best friend.

Discover

Discover the life of Irena Sendler. Google her name and read about her courageous life. Try to calculate how many lives have been saved because of her.

Capture

Capture anything you heard, saw, felt, or experienced from the day so far. Make sure to write down any dreams that you have had also.

Faith in Action

Do at least one of the following today:

1) Walk in your neighborhood and begin praying quietly for each home/apartment along your street as you walk. If you know their names, bring them before God. Ask Him to save everyone in the household and to release angels to help touch them.

2) Identify a needy area near where you live. Begin putting together a gift bag for a family, and ask the Lord what to place in it. Then ask the Lord for an apartment or home number. Find it and deliver the bag with your buddy.

Exercise

Strenuously exercise for at least thirty minutes. Set your own goal and plan for exercising. Run/walk a mile, begin lifting weights, or do aerobics. Change your eating habits, and challenge yourself physically in ways you don't normally do.

Blog

Blog the experiences you want to share at TheXJourney.com.

Journal Extraordinary

Extraordinary Journal

IN HEAVEN, *there will be hundreds of thousands of days and nights to worship God along with the myriads of angels, saints, and kneeling elders in vibrant color and light. But today, we have the privilege of focusing through the noise and darkness of the world, standing alone against the gravity of need to present a sound of unaccompanied worship that touches the heart of our Father.*

Note: Go to a new/different location to spend time with the Lord this morning (walk around outside, go to a different room, or find a rock or tree to sit beside).

Receive

Imagine Jesus hearing the words found in Mark 1:11 from the Father. Now, since you are "in Christ," imagine yourself hearing the Father saying the same words over you: "I am well pleased with you." Enjoy His pleasure with you for a few minutes.

Worship

Play your favorite song and worship the Lord along with it. Perhaps replay it a couple of times. (Suggestions: see TheXJourney.com music links.)

Pray

Pray/speak/sing in the Spirit for fifteen minutes continuously. Alternate between speaking in the Spirit to singing in the Spirit.

- Pray for the kingdom of God to come to your city, home, office, church, or neighborhood (see Matthew 6:10).
- Pray for those you know who are sick or have diseases to be healed. Speak out loud and proclaim their healing.

Proclaim

Stand on top of a piece of furniture (if safe), and proclaim out loud like you mean it, over your life today:

I am loved. I am forgiven. I know the Father of heaven and His strong Son personally. Greater is the Person inside of me than any force in the world. Jesus loves me, has set me free, and released me from all bondage. I am no longer my own, but Jesus has purchased me and I am made in His image. My mind, body, and spirit are His. I am no longer a slave to sin or fear or poverty thinking. I am not afraid any longer. I have been purchased by the living blood of Jesus and cleansed from all of my past. I have the mind of Jesus Christ.

The Holy Spirit Himself resides inside of me right now, and inside my heart is His home address. All things are becoming new in my life. I am a daughter/son of the Father of love. I have no limitations in Christ. I can do everything that Jesus did and even greater things. I have full access to the Father through Jesus, and I am seated in heaven right now with Him. I have a purpose to fulfill on this earth. Through Jesus, I have been given authority over all of the power of the enemy. I hear the voice of God, and I am an ambassador of His love to others on this earth. I am a New Covenant creature, and I will follow Jesus today into every adventure He leads me into. He has a purpose for me to fulfill. I will love the unlovable; I will see with His eyes. I will freely give away to others what He has given me. I will see the lost saved. I will see the dead raised. I will serve and obey the One I love and Who loved me first—Jesus. I am becoming His best friend.

Read

Hebrews 3 and 4.

Discover

Discover some of the history in the area where you currently live. Who settled it and why? What native tribes inhabited it previously? Google the history or ask someone who might know. Learn about cleansing the land TheXJourney.com has some suggestions on how to do this.

Faith in Action

Change the life of someone through encouragement (see Hebrews 3:13).

With your buddy, find a military veteran, a law enforcement officer, or a fireman and personally thank them for their service and selflessness. If appropriate, ask them if you can pray for and bless them, asking God for protection over their lives and His love to draw their hearts.

Capture

Capture anything you heard, saw, felt, or experienced from the day so far. Make sure to write down any dreams that you have also had.

Journal Extraordinary

Extraordinary Journal

DAY 14

THE PURPOSE *that God has for your life is surrounded by foreboding demons of fear, firing paralyzing thoughts and feelings in your direction. Reaching your divine destination means gathering up courage and facing head-on every fear that stands in your path. Your boldness to confront these fears will not only find you walking in your calling, but will also expose the façade of terror you passed through as a mask of lies (see Matthew 15:43; II Timothy 1:7; Proverbs 28:1).*

Thanks

Spend five minutes or so thanking God—not asking for anything, just thanking Him. (Thank Him for finances, resources, for your vehicle, residence, for hope, forgiveness, peace, joy, and so on.)

Pray

Pray/speak/sing in the Spirit for fifteen minutes continuously today while walking around your home or outside.

- Ask God for an interpretation to what you prayed in the Spirit. Write it down.

- Pray for the kingdom of God to come to your city, home, church, and neighborhood (see Matthew 6:10).
- Pray for those you know who are sick or have diseases to be healed. Speak out loud and proclaim their healing.

Read

Using the *Amplified* translation, read Hebrews 5 and 6.

Confront a Fear

Identify a fear in your life that terrorizes you (speaking in public, flying in an airplane, going to another nation, etc.). Write it down and make a plan to confront that fear by facing it. You have not been given a Spirit of fear, but of power, love, and a sound mind (see II Timothy 1:7). Your purpose awaits.

Discover

Learn more about the Bible. Google and discover things about William Tyndale, John Wycliffe, and the Dead Sea Scrolls.

Capture

Capture anything you heard, saw, felt, or experienced from the day so far. Make sure to write down any dreams that you have had also.

Faith in Action

Do both of the following today:

1) Think of a person who has offended or hurt you. Begin blessing them out loud, praying for great things from God to come to them. If appropriate, send them a short word of encouragement.

2) Think about the person who you feel is the furthest from salvation, the most distant from God that you know. Call them by name and bring them to the Father. Ask the Holy Spirit to pursue them and save them. Begin prophesying over their life and their destiny. "Bind" them to Jesus (see Matthew 16:19, 18:18) so they can't get away and ask the Father to draw them to Himself.

Exercise

Continue your exercise regimen Run/walk a mile, begin lifting weights, or do aerobics. Change eating habits and challenge yourself physically in ways you don't normally do.

Extraordinary Journal

Journal Extraordinary

Extraordinary Journal

Heads Up

Three-day fast this week beginning at 6 p.m. on Day 18 and concluding on Day 21 at 6 p.m.

It will take approximately 1.5 to 2 hours per day to complete everything.

Suggestions:

- Set your alarm and get up two hours earlier than you normally would.
- Continue the lifelong fast from criticism and negative talk about anyone (including yourself).
- If completing this guide as a group or church, plan a party at the end of the three day fast together.
- Note: This is the final, full week of the 22-day adventure. This week will include some new things to explore and find out about God. I believe this week will also include unforeseen breakthroughs for you spiritually and physically.

Extraordinary Journal

the Extraordinary Journey

FLUSH ALL OF THE IMAGES *in your mind of how you think things will turn out in your life—marriage, ministry, career. Then, with your eyes fixed upon Jesus alone, follow Him wherever He goes, partnering with Him in His missions, loving those in your life extravagantly. While enjoying the journey, He will create a masterpiece behind you of His will fulfilled in your life from the palette of your mistakes, service, and the love you have given away to the least of these along the way.*

Receive

Imagine Jesus hearing the words found in Mark 1:11 from His Father. Since you are "in Christ," imagine yourself hearing your Father saying these same words over you—"I am well pleased with you." Enjoy His pleasure with you for a few minutes. Receive His love down into the deepest part of your heart today.

Commune

With juice or wine (if twenty-one or older) and bread (or crackers), commune with Jesus and remember Him. Receive all that He has for you—all of His power and love. Exchange with Him (see John 6 and I Corinthians 11:23-26).

Create

The most creative Person in the universe lives inside of you. Ask Him for creative ideas, then create something (write a poem, write a song, construct something, draw a prophetic picture, paint a scene, capture an image of creation, and so on).

Dress Up

Put on all of the armor described in Ephesians 6:13-17. Read it and put on each one for all that is ahead today.

Pray

Pray/speak/sing in the Spirit for fifteen minutes every day (at one time).

- Pray the Lord's Prayer found in Matthew 6:9-13.
- For five minutes or so, pray for the lost (unsaved relatives, co-workers, prisoners, people in your neighborhood, and so on).
- Pray a few minutes for the Jewish people, for Jerusalem, and the nation of Israel (see Psalm 122:6).

Proclaim

Speak these verses out loud. Say them like you mean them. Engage your spirit in: II Corinthians 5:17 and I Peter 1:3-4.

Identify an area in your life that you don't like and proclaim out loud that it is changing now, lining up with the kingdom. Tell sickness or ailment to leave your body.

Discover

1) Find a dream or prophetic word that God has given to you in the past and ask the Lord to speak to you about it, help interpret it for you, and re-engage in reminding the Lord of the promise in it.

2) Go to tinyurl.com/dynamiccell and discover the incredible creative organization of the physical foundation of you. Also, see a cell at work, realizing that God has formed you beyond comprehension: tinyurl.com/InnerCell.

Read

Colossians 1 and 2.

Faith in Action

Step out in faith and do at least one of the following today:

1) Share a testimony of something that God has done for you with an unsaved neighbor, friend, relative, or co-worker (when you were healed, when God provided a breakthrough for you, when He answered a prayer, when you participated in a miracle, etc.).

2) Invite an unsaved family or couple in your neighborhood over for dinner. Be kind, spoil them, and ask about them. Don't preach to them.

Fast

Continue to fast from all criticism, negativity, and thinking about/dwelling on anything from the past that was hurtful. Bless all who have ever done you harm.

Capture

Capture anything you heard, saw, felt, and experienced. Remember to capture your dreams and visions also.

Blog

Blog the experiences you want to share at TheXJourney.com.

Extraordinary Journal

Extraordinary Journal

DAY 16

THE NORMAL ACTIVITIES in our daily lives bring us near strategically placed burning bushes. Papa leaves these mysterious clues out in the open to see if His kids want to play, desiring to get our attention so He can reveal our parts in delivering nations. Any clue that tugs on our curiosity invites the busy to turn aside and discover with kid-like wonder, purposes, and journeys that we didn't know existed.

Receive

Picture yourself at the bottom of the waterfall of Him, and He is pouring Himself and everything He has into you, filling you to the brink. Receive Him and imagine yourself filled to overflowing with Him (see Ephesians 5:18).

Pray

Pray/speak/sing in the Spirit for fifteen minutes every day (at one time). Do this while walking.

- Pray the Lord's Prayer found in Matthew 6:9-13.
- For five minutes or so, pray for the lost (unsaved relatives, co-workers, prisoners, people in your neighborhood, and so on).

- Pray a few minutes for the Jewish people, for Jerusalem, and for the nation of Israel (see Psalm 122:6).

Proclaim

Stand up and say the following out loud (more than once if you want to):

Jesus has given me <u>everything</u> pertaining to life and godliness. I have been crucified with Jesus, and I lack nothing in Him. I am a joint heir with Jesus. Through the currency of faith, I receive all that He has for me now. His power flows through my veins. Devil, I push you off of all the resources God has for me. I rebuke you and kick you off of the seed I have sown in the past. I remove you from my home, my health, my finances, my mind, and my dreams. In Jesus' name, be removed from the promises God has given to me and my family. My bloodline is cleansed and God is my inheritance and my portion, and that portion is awesome. The prophetic promises that God has given to me throughout my life are still valid. I hold onto these promises as personal invitations from God to keep moving forward until they are fulfilled. I will not dwell in the past but in Jesus. The kingdom of God is near and within me. Living water is flowing from my inner man to bring life to others. I am full of the Holy Spirit and the love of God.

Discover

1) Pay attention to billboards, scraps of paper on the ground, road signs, and headlines. See if the Lord will speak to you through the contemporary things in life and be expectant to hear Him spark a new journey of discovery.

2) Find a dream or prophetic word that God has given to you in the past and ask the Lord to speak to you about it, help interpret it for you, and re-engage in reminding the Lord of the promise in it.

Read

Colossians 3 and 4.

Memorize

Galatians 2:20.

Faith in Action

Build your confidence and faith by doing at least one of following with your buddy today:

1) Go up to someone unsaved (if it is obvious) and tell him or her that they are loved. Ask him or her if they have met the Lover of their soul yet. Share Jesus with him or her.
2) With a partner, pay for a taxi ride somewhere, and share the gospel message of hope, life, healing, and forgiveness with the taxi driver. Lead him to Jesus if possible.

Breaking the Cycle

Continue to fast from all criticism, negativity, and thinking about/dwelling on anything from the past that was hurtful.

Capture

Capture anything you heard, saw, felt, and experienced. Remember to journal your dreams and visions also.

Serve

Give ten to fifteen minutes to someone to help them in any way (washing dishes, a massage for your spouse, cleaning someone's car, run errands, and so on).

Journal Extraordinary

Extraordinary Journal

DAY 17

WE ACT LIKE PAGANS in a crisis, only one out of a crowd is daring enough to bank his faith in the character of God.

~Oswald Chambers

Receive

Stand at the bottom of the waterfall of His power and grace. Receive as He pours Himself and everything He has into you, filling you up. Receive Him and imagine yourself being filled to overflowing with Him (see Ephesians 5:18).

Pray

Pray/speak/sing in the Spirit for fifteen minutes every day (at one time).

- Pray the Lord's Prayer found in Matthew 6:9-13.
- For five minutes or so, pray for the lost (unsaved relatives, co-workers, prisoners, people in your neighborhood, and so on).
- Pray a few minutes for the Jewish people, for Jerusalem, and for the nation of Israel (see Psalm 122:6).

Proclaim

Speak II Corinthians 5:17 and I Peter 1:3-4 out loud. Say them like you mean them. Engage your spirit.

Stand up and say the following out loud (more than once if you want to):

Jesus has given me <u>everything</u> pertaining to life and godliness. I have been crucified with Jesus, and I lack nothing in Him. I am a joint heir with Jesus. Through the currency of faith, I receive all that He has for me now. His power flows through my veins. Devil, I push you off of all the resources God has for me. I rebuke you and kick you off of the seed I have sown in the past. I remove you from my home, my health, my finances, my mind, and my dreams. In Jesus' name, be removed from the promises God has given to me and my family. My bloodline is cleansed and God is my inheritance and my portion, and that portion is awesome. The prophetic promises that God has given to me throughout my life are still valid. I hold onto these promises as personal invitations from God to keep moving forward until they are fulfilled. I will not dwell in the past but in Jesus. The kingdom of God is near and within me. Living water is flowing from my inner man to bring life to others. I am full of the Holy Spirit and the love of God.

Dance

Play a favorite song on an audio player, close the blinds to the house, and dance with all of your might. Let loose. Repeat and go for it again. Read II

Samuel 6:14. (I suggest "Dress Us Up" by John Mark McMillan.)

Discover

Google/discover from *Christian History Magazine* as much as you can about Jon Amos Comenius. Find out what "labyrinth of the world, paradise of the heart" is about.

Read

Ephesians 1 and 2.

Memorize

John 8:12.

Faith in Action

Build your spiritual muscle of faith by doing at least one of the following today:

1) Get in line at a coffee shop and buy coffee for the person behind you, then encourage him or her by sharing hope and life when they ask why you are doing this.

2) Get in line at a store and ask the Lord for a word of knowledge (healing) for the checkout clerk. At checkout, give them the word and pray for them, proclaiming their healing.

Fast

Continue to fast from all criticism, negativity, and thinking about/dwelling on anything from the past that was hurtful.

Capture

Capture anything you heard, saw, felt, experienced. Remember to journal your night dreams and visions also.

Exercise

Set a goal and plan for exercising. Run/walk a mile, begin lifting weights, or do aerobics. Change your eating habits, and challenge yourself physically in ways you don't normally do.

Blog

Blog the experiences you want to share at TheXJourney.com

Extraordinary Journal

Extraordinary Journal

DAY 18

OUR JOB IS NOT TO *convict people of sin, but to lavish the kindness of God upon everything that breathes. His kindness delivered through us has a thousand times more power than condescending truth or self-righteous preaching. The kindness of God has the power to penetrate the hardest of hearts, unravel the most twisted of minds, and draw the distant near.*

Note: Today at 6 p.m., begin your three-day fast that will end with a celebration. May there be "grace, grace" on your fasting and may each meal be replaced with tasting and swallowing the goodness of God, getting full on His invisible morsels (see Psalm 34:8; John 4:32).

I encourage you to change your routine and find a different location to spend time with the Lord this morning (walk outside, go to a different room, or get into your tub).

Receive/Filled with the Spirit

Before doing anything else in the day, come before the Lord and receive a brand new infilling of the Holy Spirit. Picture yourself at the bottom of the waterfall of Him. He is pouring Himself and everything He has into you, filling you up. Receive Him and imagine yourself being filled to overflowing with Him (see Ephesians 5:18).

Pray

Pray/speak/sing in the Spirit for fifteen minutes every day (at one time).

- Pray the Lord's Prayer found in Matthew 6:9-13.
- For five minutes or so, pray for the lost (unsaved relatives, co-workers, prisoners, people in your neighborhood, and so on).
- Pray a few minutes for the Jewish people, for Jerusalem, and the nation of Israel (see Psalm 122:6).

Proclaim

Speak II Corinthians 5:17 and I Peter 1:3-4 out loud. Say them like you mean them. Engage your spirit.

Then stand up and say this out loud (more than once if you want to):

Jesus has given me <u>everything</u> pertaining to life and godliness. I have been crucified with Jesus, and I lack nothing in Him. I am a joint heir with Jesus. Through the currency of faith, I receive all that He has for me now. His power flows through my veins. Devil, I push you off of all the resources God has for me. I rebuke you and kick you off of the seed I have sown in the past. I remove you from my home, my health, my finances, my mind, and my dreams. In Jesus' name, be removed from the promises God has given to me and my family. My bloodline is cleansed and God is my *inheritance and my portion, and that portion is awesome. The prophetic promises that God has given to me throughout my life are still valid. I hold onto these promises as personal invitations from God to keep moving forward until they are fulfilled. I will not dwell in the past but in Jesus. The kingdom of God is near and within me. Living water is flowing from my inner man to bring life to others. I am full of the Holy Spirit and the love of God.*

Wait/Listen

Wait on God without praying or straying for ten minutes every day. Just listen and be still . . . Quiet your soul . . . Look and see . . . Watch and wait….

Capture

Immediately after waiting, capture anything you heard, saw, felt, and experienced. Remember to capture your dreams and visions also.

Discover

1) Google and discover as much as you can about a twentieth century hero, Gladys Aylward.
2) Look up, find, and visit a gelato shop and taste a few different flavors to discover your favorite.
3) Go to TheXJourney.com and watch some of the universe by watching the universe videos.

Faith in Action

Build your spiritual muscle of faith by doing both of the following today.

1) Ask the Lord for a ten-digit phone number that you are unfamiliar with, and then ask Him for an encouraging word for the person. Call the number and give the encouraging word. If the first number you call doesn't work, ask for another, and call it until you connect with someone.

2) Walk around the four corners of your home (inside) and apply the blood of Jesus by faith, breaking the spiritual power of anything else in the atmosphere. Claim your home as a place for the Holy Spirit to dwell.

Read

Galatians 1 and 2.

Memorize

John 8:12.

Fast

Continue fasting from food and from thinking/dwelling upon anything from the past that was hurtful, from all criticism of yourself or of others. Ask God to forgive you of all criticism you have ever said about anyone else.

Blog

Blog the experiences you want to share at TheXJourney.com.

Journal Extraordinary

Extraordinary Journal

DAVID DANCED *with "all his might" and God loved it. David wasn't a trained dancer participating in a beautifully choreographed performance, but rather a son who would rather act a celebratory fool than live without the presence of God.*

Receive/Filled with the Spirit

He is pouring Himself and everything He has into you, filling you to the brink. Receive Him and imagine yourself filled to overflowing with Him. Read Acts 13:52.

Commune

With juice or wine (if in the U.S., must be twenty-one or older) and bread (or crackers), commune with Jesus and remember Him. Read John 6:26-64 and I Corinthians 11:23-26 as you partake.

Thanks

Spend five minutes or so thanking God (thank Him for all who are in authority over you, for difficulties, for discipline, for the nations, for Israel, and so on).

Pray

Pray/speak/sing in the Spirit for fifteen minutes every day (at one time).

- Pray the Lord's Prayer found in Matthew 6:9-13.
- For five minutes or so, pray for the lost (unsaved relatives, co-workers, prisoners, people in your neighborhood, and so on). Call them by name and bind them to Jesus (see Matthew 16:19).
- Pray a few minutes for the Jewish people, for Jerusalem, and the nation of Israel (see Psalm 122:6).

Dance

Play a favorite song on an audio player, close the blinds to the house, and dance with all of your might. Let loose. Repeat and go for it until King David would have been impressed (see II Samuel 6:14).

Laugh

Think back to a time in the last several years when you laughed the hardest. Allow yourself to laugh again. If you can't think of anything, imagine being your neighbor and having just seen you dance like a wild person through the blinds.

Proclaim

Speak these verses II Corinthians 5:17 and I Peter 1:3-4 out loud. Say them like you mean them. Engage your spirit.

Stand up and say this out loud (more than once if you want to):

the Extraordinary Journey

Jesus has given me <u>everything</u> pertaining to life and godliness. I have been crucified with Jesus, and I lack nothing in Him. I am a joint heir with Jesus. Through the currency of faith, I receive all that He has for me now. His power flows through my veins. Devil, I push you off of all the resources God has for me. I rebuke you and kick you off of the seed I have sown in the past. I remove you from my home, my health, my finances, my mind, and my dreams. In Jesus' name, be removed from the promises God has given to me and my family. My bloodline is cleansed and God is my inheritance and my portion, and that portion is awesome. The prophetic promises that God has given to me throughout my life are still valid. I hold onto these promises as personal invitations from God to keep moving forward until they are fulfilled. I will not dwell in the past but in Jesus. The kingdom of God is near and within me. Living water is flowing from my inner man to bring life to others. I am full of the Holy Spirit and the love of God.

Capture

Capture anything you heard, saw, felt, and experienced. Take a few minutes to write the Lord a "thank you" note in your journal.

Read

Galatians 2 and 4.

Memorize

Acts 16:31.

Exercise

Exercise for at least forty-five minutes. Set your own goals and plan. Run/walk a mile, begin lifting weights, or do aerobics. Change your eating habits and challenge yourself physically in ways you don't normally do.

Breaking the Cycle

Continue fasting from all criticism and all negativity about anyone. Fast from thinking/dwelling upon anything from the past that was hurtful.

Journal Extraordinary

Extraordinary Journal

DAY 20

ONE OF THE STARK CONTRASTS between how the devil and God communicate is that "the devil drives" and "the Lord leads." The enemy operates like a used car salesmen, pressuring and pushing us to do things. In an opposite Spirit, the Lord leads by invitation and peace. Our answer to pressures of every variety should be an instant "no." The invitations of God may cost us everything, but they never come with religious pressure and are never pushy. God is looking for adventurous sons and daughters who want to be with Him, not coerced laborers forced to toe the line.

Dive into the River of His Delight

Jump into the river of God, diving into His delight, His rest, His freedom, and His intense love for you. Believe that what He says about you is true.

Worship

Play your favorite song and worship the Lord along with it. Perhaps replay it a couple of times.

Pray

Pray/speak/sing in the Spirit for fifteen minutes (at one time).

- Pray the Lord's prayer found in Matthew 6:9-13.

- For five minutes or so pray for the lost (unsaved relatives, co-workers, prisoners, people in our neighborhood, etc.).
- Pray a few minutes for the Jewish people, for Jerusalem, and the nation of Israel (see Psalm 122:6).

Proclaim

Speak II Corinthians 5:17 and I Peter 1:3-4 out loud. Say them like you mean them. Engage your spirit.

Stand up and say this out loud (more than once if you want to):

Jesus has given me <u>everything</u> pertaining to life and godliness. I have been crucified with Jesus, and I lack nothing in Him. I am a joint heir with Jesus. Through the currency of faith, I receive all that He has for me now. His power flows through my veins. Devil, I push you off of all the resources God has for me. I rebuke you and kick you off of the seed I have sown in the past. I remove you from my home, my health, my finances, my mind, and my dreams. In Jesus' name, be removed from the promises God has given to me and my family. My bloodline is cleansed and God is my inheritance and my portion, and that portion is awesome. The prophetic promises that God has given to me throughout my life are still valid. I hold onto these promises as personal invitations from God to keep moving forward until they are fulfilled. I will not dwell in the past but in Jesus. The kingdom of God is near and within me. Living water is flowing from my inner man to bring life to others. I am full of the Holy Spirit and the love of God.

Wait/Listen

Wait on God without praying or straying for ten minutes every day. Just listen and be still . . . Look and see . . . Watch and wait. . . .

Capture

Immediately after waiting, capture anything you heard, saw, felt, and experienced. Remember to capture your dreams and visions also.

Discover

Discover what "atonement" means and what it does for you.

Faith in Action

Build your spiritual muscle of faith by doing one of the following today:

1) Call someone that you don't know very well in your church and pray and encourage him or her over the phone—not correcting or giving anything negative at all. Our guide is found in I Corinthians 14:3.
2) Practice multiplying food. Take food to the needy and pray over it. Then begin giving it out and see if it multiplies.

Read

Galatians 5 and 6.

Serve

Give fifteen minutes to someone to help them in any way (washing dishes, a massage for your spouse, cleaning someone's car, run errands, and so on).

Breaking the Cycle

Continue fasting from all criticism and all negativity about anyone. Fast from thinking/dwelling upon anything from the past that was hurtful.

Blog

Blog the experiences you want to share at TheXJourney.com.

Journal Extraordinary

Extraordinary Journal

THE HARDSHIPS, *difficulties, and losses in life can become catapults launching us into new authority if we don't provide the ship of bitterness safe harbor in our soul through the process.*

Note: Good morning! I hope you slept well. I know it feels like your stomach is eating itself by now. Tonight we eat and enjoy eating again. Let's make the most of this day by surrendering our all, using our weakness to let Him know how much we need Him in our lives.

Commune

With juice or wine (if in the U.S., must be twenty-one or older) and bread (or crackers)—not a whole loaf, even though you may want to—commune with Jesus and remember Him. Receive all that He has for you—all of His power and love. Exchange with Him. Read John 6 and Corinthians 11:23-26.

Thanks

Spend five minutes or so thanking God—not asking for anything, just thanking Him. Thank Him for all who are in authority over you, for difficulties, for discipline, for the nations, for Israel. Thank Him for the power of the resurrection for food and provision, and so on.

Pray

Pray/speak/sing in the Spirit for fifteen minutes (at one time).

- Pray the Lord's Prayer found in Matthew 6:9-13.
- Pray for justice in our nation, for unjust laws to be overturned, and help for the unborn.
- Pray a few minutes for our nation—its leadership and governing bodies.

Dance

Though your body may feel weak, worship. Play a favorite song, close the blinds to the house, and dance with all of your might. Let loose. See II Samuel 6:14.

Proclaim

Speak II Corinthians 5:17 and I Peter 1:3-4 out loud. Say them like you mean them. Engage your spirit.

Stand up and say this out loud (more than once if you want to):

Jesus has given me <u>everything</u> pertaining to life and godliness. I have been crucified with Jesus, and I lack nothing in Him. I am a joint heir with Jesus. Through the currency of faith, I receive all that He has for me now. His power flows through my veins. Devil, I push you off of all the resources God has for me. I rebuke you and kick you off of the seed I have sown in the past. I remove you from my home, my health, my finances, my mind, and my dreams. In Jesus' name, be removed from the promises God has given to me and my family. My bloodline is cleansed and God is my inheritance and my portion, and that portion is awesome. The prophetic promises that God has given to me throughout *my life are still valid. I hold onto these promises as personal invitations from God to keep moving forward until they are fulfilled. I will not dwell in the past but in Jesus. The kingdom of God is near and within me. Living water is flowing from my inner man to bring life to others. I am full of the Holy Spirit and the love of God.*

Wait/Listen

Wait on God without praying or straying for ten minutes. Just listen and be still . . . Look and see . . . Watch and wait….

Capture

Immediately after waiting, journal anything you heard, saw, felt, and experienced. Remember to capture your dreams and visions also.

Discover

Discover and learn more about angels from the Scriptures (what their purposes and missions are, and so on).

Faith in Action

Build your spiritual muscle of faith by choosing to do one of the following today:

1) Ask God to place someone in your church fellowship on your heart and then ask Him for a Scripture and prophetic/encouraging word for them. Write it down and give it to them the next time you see them.

2) Begin to raise money for a family or some type of cause. Map out a plan and lavish on that family or help the cause.

Read

Philippians 1, 2, and 3.

Blog

Blog the experiences you want to share at TheXJourney.com.

Challenge

Pick a ministry to serve within in your church and get involved (if not involved already, try to get involved at least once per month).

Buy a journal and continue journaling every day. Start a dream journal to capture the dreams that the Lord gives you in the night.

Journal Extraordinary

Extraordinary Journal

DAY 22

THE FINAL DAY *of this short journey is simply a springboard into thousands of journeys yet to come.*

Note: We will be doing something entirely different on this final day.

Reflect

Take a minute and reflect on this 22-day journey. What were the highlights and what was the most difficult?

Become a Storyteller

Jesus told forty unique stories to people, most of them describing aspects of the kingdom. These stories stirred curiosity, were compelling, and people could identify with the everyday elements Jesus described. Create a short story (400 words or less) in contemporary language that describes something about the kingdom, the purpose of mankind on the earth, the love of God, etc.

Practice telling it and become a storyteller that inspires and captivates without religious words.

Dream About the Future

If you could do anything, and money was no object, had unlimited talent and resources, and you were not afraid of anything, anyone, or any place, *what would you do*? Would you move somewhere, start a business, marry someone, serve in an orphanage, go to college, write a book, stand up for justice, help a tribe, or save a nation? Jesus said that nothing or no thing is impossible with God (see Luke 1:37). *If you can dream it, if the desire is in your heart (particularly as it relates to helping free others), you can do it.* Write down this dream of yours.

Move Forward

Skyscrapers are built one beam at a time, and dreams are fulfilled one step at a time. Take the dream you've written down and make a plan to take the first step toward it. Do some research, and then learn and pray about how to move forward. Take a step of faith and do what you've never done before. I suspect that you will find doors of opportunity and inspiration open before you. Be prepared for the long haul and don't quit. The Lord may redirect and clarify your dream along the way, but keep moving forward toward it.

Celebrate: see Launch Point, pg. 172

Gather together with others to creatively celebrate the magnificence of God.

Parting Thoughts

Contrary to the well-known saying, not all "good things" come to an end. Some good things actually go from good to spectacular. This is your calling.

the Extraordinary Journey

The short journey you have just completed was simply a taste of what you can have every day for the remainder of your life. You can live knowing you are loved, and you can walk in abiding fellowship and power as Jesus walked. Your journey isn't 22 days long, it's 22 trillion. Now that you have tasted of new experiences in God, I encourage you to go from this taste to a lifetime of discovering and exploring. I encourage you to make a list of every fear you have ever had and begin confronting all of them, step-by-step. I encourage you to dream bigger than you have ever dreamed and make your own Faith in Action list of things to do in your city, nation, or another nation.

Since nothing is impossible with God and He resides in you, there is nothing impossible for you to do in Him.

Extraordinary Journal

Journal Extraordinary

Extraordinary Journal

Launch Points

the Extraordinary Journey

Launch Point: Receiving

Within the New Covenant, we are recipients of all that Jesus purchased. In fact, the gospel message is "good news" about what has already been done, not what we have to do. We are sons and daughters, not slaves of sin toiling to earn a wage. Sadly, most believers feel distant from God—unless they are in a worship service or have done something good. Most believers inwardly feel a sense of not deserving the presence of God every moment of the day. Many of us pray, read, and do good things with the hope that we *will* be pleasing unto God, so He in turn, will be obliged to do good things for us. This mindset and feeling is the result of being under the influence of a religious spirit and an Old Covenant mentality.

NEW COVENANT REALITY is the exact opposite. The promise of the New Covenant is that we who believe *have already been* literally transferred and transported out from the kingdom of darkness. You have been placed within a brilliant kingdom, ruled by the Son who is in love with you and lives within you. The blood of Jesus makes us acceptable, not your effort. You have already been approved, paid for, considered adequate, pleasing and acceptable to God long ago—on the day you believed. You are a cared for child of His, not a stranger. You don't have to, and cannot earn, His presence. Jesus earned it for us and we are in Him now (see Acts 17:28).

In the kingdom ruled by Jesus, you no longer have to strive and labor to become good enough to receive

the Extraordinary Journey

love, forgiveness, and intimacy with God. Whether you realize it or not, you are seated with Him in heavenly places right now—the best seat in the entire universe! In the kingdom where you now reside, you are a son and a daughter who has been paid for, adopted, accepted, and loved without measure—this moment—with no begging or pleading for attention any longer. No good work will outweigh your sins and no effort will finally get His attention, which has been on you from before the earth was formed. He is already crazy in love with you, and you are already an heir in His kingdom. You are royalty, and you are forgiven.

Consider the Father's pleasure that was communicated to Jesus at the Jordan River. Jesus heard **"My Son, in whom I am well pleased" (see Matthew 12:18)** before He did one miracle, before He gave one message, or before He became successful or endured the cross. He received His Father's words of love and affirmation prior to doing ministry or anything of merit. We are sons and daughters of His also. He is pleased with you because you are His.

Your new job as a son or daughter is to *receive and to believe* (see John 6:29). Receiving the love of your Father in vast quantities on a daily basis is a part of your inheritance and a practical way to live free.

As a believer and a child of God, you get to receive, bathe, and linger in the love of God whenever you want to. The practice of this receiving will begin to unravel the religious mindsets and feelings of distance from God.

the Extraordinary Journey

Launch Point: Exchanging

The essence of the Christian life is that Jesus has done everything for us. We have done nothing, yet we get to receive and partake of all His lavish benefits.

The antithesis to the spirit of religion is *exchanging*. Exchanging is the action we made the day we met Jesus, when we exchanged our SIN FOR HIS FORGIVENESS. Beyond the day of our salvation, exchanging is a way of living that we must learn to operate in as effortlessly as breathing for the remainder of our lives.

Most believers live daily with a certain level of condemnation, regret, and guilt. Most believers carry around a weight of care, concern, and anxiety. According to the words of Jesus, none of this should be. His blood personally paid for all of the condemnation, regret, guilt, care, concern, and anxiety we have ever had. The way we unload these thoughts and feelings is by a simple act of faith—we make the great exchange as often as we need to make it.

Jesus said, **"Come to Me, all who are weary and heavy-laden, and I will give you rest. Take My yoke upon you and learn from Me, for I am gentle and humble in heart, and you will find rest for your souls" (Matthew 11:28-29)**.

The astounding, standing invitation of Jesus is to make an exchange with Him any time, all the time—our sin for His forgiveness, our guilt and shame for His innocence and freedom, our heavy concerns for His featherweight joy. All of this is done by simple faith. Learning to quickly exchange our bad feelings, confusing emotions, and junk for His love will result in freedom and joy, which is the pathway to a healthy life.

Religion adds pressure, reinforcing the weight of our filth and ineptitude. Jesus is the opposite. He removes the weights and gives us Himself instead—our minds for His mind (see I Corinthians 2:16), our feelings of hopelessness for His confidence and love, and our weakness for His strength.

Similar to the crazy notion that a kid with a beat-up, dingy paper airplane could approach a NASA official and exchange his paper plane for a billion dollar space shuttle, the kids of God get to approach Him as often as we like, and make a far greater exchange. We get the ridiculously real, seemingly too-good-to-be-true, lottery-like exchange of trading away all of our crud and sins for the boundless Holy Spirit without measure. We get to climb into forgiveness by the truckload, drink joy by the gallon, and swim in the rivers of freedom. Jesus is looking to trade. He's interested in every one of His loved ones coming to Him with any and every grimy, pitiful, and dark thing, so that He can reach into the treasure chest of Himself and give us all that we need—at any time, any place, and always without cost.

Humility is taking advantage of this, the best deal in the universe, and learning to become a frequent exchanger with God. Pride is the pathway whereby we carry the weight and the burden. It's working up more effort and trying harder to do what has already been done by Jesus two thousand years ago. The exchanger finds grace and rest while the proud finds opposition to the One who gives freely and wants His kids to enjoy and give that enjoyment away to others.

Launch Point: Communion

Jesus left us a tangible reminder of His hardship and torture in the form of something we would enjoy—bread and wine. This is a message in itself. He did all of the work, paid the price, and did the sweating so that we wouldn't have to. We get to enjoy, while remembering what He did through His amazing love. He said that He was the living bread that came down out of heaven and gave life to the world (see John 6). He said that His blood was TRUE DRINK and His flesh was TRUE FOOD, not just a memory of manna, but living bread that gives life when we consume, swallow, and enjoy.

God is meant for us to enjoy, not just to serve. We were created for fellowship with Him personally and communion, or *union,* with Him at His table is something we not only get to do here, but we will get to eat at His table eternally with Him.

Communion was never intended to become a ritual of works, but rather an enjoyable meal of intimacy and remembrance. Communion is an invitation to the table of grace and life.

Just as food, tasted by our tongues and swallowed, travels to areas hidden within our bodies, so does the Spirit of God fill our inner most parts with Himself, reaching every hidden portion of our beings. Included with partaking of the elements is receiving and ingesting the wonderful Spirit of God within us, "tasting and seeing that He is good."

Launch Point: Thanks

The will of God is for us to **"give thanks" (see I Thessalonians 5:18).** Thankfulness is the opposite of complaining and grumbling. Thanks will OPEN WIDE THE GATES, which changes our perspective and thanks is an open rebuke to a poverty mindset.

King David, a man after God's own heart, was a man of thanks. Numerous times he was recorded giving thanks or encouraging others to give thanks. King David thanked God in all kinds of circumstances—difficult or good.

Jesus, before multiplying bread and fish, looked to heaven and thanked His Father for the little that He had in His hands. Soon, little became loads. Thanks has that type of quality, a generosity of appreciation suddenly becoming more for us to give away.

A thankful person is a free person. When a man or woman can thank without resentment, this is a sign they have forgiven and been freed from the bondage of their hurts. When you and I can thank God for everything, the devil loses traction and entry points into our lives.

Thankfulness is a sign that the enemy is defeated in our hearts and a declaration of the goodness and lavishness of God, who is working all things out for our good. Thanks is a mark of a mature believer just as complaining and grumbling are the brand of immaturity. Practicing thanks in the morning, in the evening, in the tough times and in the easy, when I feel lousy and when I feel great, when I'm spoken well of and when I'm accused, is one of the keys of victory and demonstration of the kingdom.

If appreciation for provision touches the heart of a father or a mother, it certainly reaches the heart of God. Appreciation and thanks are freewill love letters sent from here to heaven, and not one of them is thrown aside. The sacrifice of Jesus is worthy of unending thanksgiving from the earth, in every season and every trial.

Launch Point: Prayer

Prayer is multifaceted communication with an unlimited Father and Son (see I John 1:3). In the Scriptures, PRAYER TAKES VARIOUS FORMS and has various purposes. Just as God is without limit, communication with Him is unlimited and varied.

While Jesus taught His disciples to **"Pray. . . in this way" (see Matthew 6:9-13),** Jude talked about praying in the Holy Spirit to "build ourselves up on our most Holy faith" (see Jude 20) and Paul talked about praying in **"tongues more than you all" (see I Corinthians 14:18).**

Prayer can be a thought toward God; it can be in song form; it can be uttered as a cry or spoken in an unlearned tongue. In every and all ways, prayer is the wonderful language of expressing our hearts toward our God and participating with His indwelling Holy Spirit in voicing languages only He knows, releasing heaven to change things we cannot.

Rather than an obligatory ritual, prayer is an inviting conversation, a creative poem, and sometimes a desperate request. When we determine to pray for certain things or in certain ways, the Lord helps our weakness and assists us in praying to and with Him. By faith we put His word into words and our requests into songs to Him; and He, from within us, unites our words with His.

Prayer is not meant to be **"meaningless repetition" (see Matthew 6:7)** or a thousand loud words for others to notice. The Pharisees prayed for attention, prayed as a formula, and Jesus warned against these types of prayers. Instead, prayer is the access of sons and daughters who have the attention of their Father to share with Him, declaring His purposes and expressing their love for Him. Prayer is meant to be enjoyed.

Launch Point: Filled with the Holy Spirit

One of the specific purposes of Jesus coming to earth and then returning to heaven from His successful mission was to send the HOLY SPIRIT FROM HEAVEN to live permanently within the heirs of salvation. The person of the Holy Spirit was intentionally sent to dwell within and help us.

Through ministering to others, living life, and expending energy on the earth, I've recognized that I need multiple replenishings of the Holy Spirit. Just as my natural body requires water daily, my spiritual man thirsts for continued drinks and refillings of the Spirit sent from heaven. Ephesians 5:18 says "Don't be drunk with wine, but be filled with the Holy Spirit." A natural person is capable of getting drunk often with wine, even daily (although the Bible says not to); likewise, we can be filled often with the Holy Spirit, even daily.

One day a mentor of mine looked at me and then mentioned that I was running on empty with the Holy Spirit. When he said that, I didn't feel condemned, but rather it confirmed how I felt internally. With spiritual eyes, he could see my drained spirit and asked me if I wanted to get filled back up. I said yes! He then shared with me one way that he had learned to "drink in the Holy Spirit." He said that he imagined himself at the bottom of a waterfall with his mouth wide open and the Holy Spirit rushing into him until he was full and overflowing. By faith, he began to do this in my presence and received a drink from heaven. Through the years since then, I have often imagined the person of the Holy Spirit filling and refilling me. John the Baptist said that Jesus would give the Holy Spirit **"without measure" (see John 3:34).** If we are to

"taste and see that the Lord is good" (see Psalm 34:8), we can certainly "drink" of His Spirit in huge amounts without measure.

Launch Point: Access

When Jesus tore the veil in two, removing the separation between God and man, He purchased eternal access for us. This access doesn't just apply to our next life, but access to heaven and the presence of the Father while we are here on earth.

Access is a mark of both FAVOR AND RESPONSIBILITY. Favor, in that we have been given unmerited favor through Jesus to live near and approach the Father. Responsibility, in that life isn't just for us to enjoy, but also for us to use our access on behalf of others. Just as Queen Esther used her access with the king to leverage help for her people, doing the will of God, we are encouraged to **"come boldly to the throne of grace" (see Hebrews 4:16 NKJV)** and to **"not merely look out for your own personal interests, but also for the interests of others" (see Philippians 2:4).**

Access is potential leverage on behalf of others. Jesus is the supreme example of this. Having access to His Father, He showed us what He is like. He shared with us the bounty that His access affords. We have the privilege of doing the same. Freely, we can give away what we have been given, discovering revelation and sharing it with others to help them. We can approach the Father and bring the name of a needy one along with us, requesting help on their behalf. We can ask God for just one kind thought of His to give away to someone else so they can hear of His kindness or access the healing of the Master for someone who needs a touch.

Launch Point: Discovering

The closest person to ever walk with God has only experienced a miniscule fraction of a God that is larger than the universe. Our life here on this earth and in the life to come will forever be a DISCOVERY UPON DISCOVERY of who He is, what He is like, and how He does things. As His children, one of our privileges is to spend the rest of our lives discovering more things about Him, like eager treasure hunters that are never satisfied.

Discovery can take many forms. The miracle of life, the internal desires of our children, the vastness of our solar system, and the unending layers of revelation attached to every verse of Scripture are waiting to be discovered and explored. God is the ultimate pioneer, and we are made in His image. We are creative pioneers who will forever get to explore the wonders of creation, the depths of His love, and the revelation hidden in His creation.

Discovering new things is like the sun melting away the mold of the mundane. The Holy Spirit searches the deep things of God and He lives within us to reveal the hidden mysteries of Christ to us (see Colossians 2:2-3).

Launch Point: Read

The foundation of our lives should be upon the magnificent WORDS OF GOD which were collected throughout thousands of years, from numerous authors and preserved against enormous odds. Many have lost their lives and risked all to present these words to us in black, white, and red. The collection of poems, history, songs, stories, and love letters expressed on paper provide us with an unparalleled masterpiece that should incite a hunger within us to have these Words in our minds and hearts, pouring back to Him through our prayers and encouragement to others.

There are different ways to read and study the Bible. Some read it with the mindset of performing a duty, scratching it off a checklist. Some read it to gain information and knowledge that supports their viewpoint. Still others eat the words on the pages as if it were bread coming down from heaven and a necessary meal that becomes part of them.

Jeremiah said **"Your words were found and I ate them, and Your words became for me a joy and the delight of my heart" (see Jeremiah 15:16).**

I believe there is no better way to read the compilation of love letters from God called the Scriptures, than to consume them and let them become a joy and delight to our hearts. This means that instead of reading for information only, we allow His Words to become a part of us, changing our viewpoints, and cleansing us from the inside.

Jesus said to His disciples that they were **"already clean because of the word which I have spoken to you" (see John 15:3).** The Words of God are cleansing agents with transforming qualities as we ingest and meditate on what we have consumed. There is also a steadiness and a solidness, a calmness and a peace, within those who have made His Word a priority to live by.

Pride can result from reading only for the sake of knowledge, but joy and delight, steadfastness and faith, result as we taste, see, and swallow Him and His **"sweeter than honey" (see Psalm 119:103)** Words.

Launch Point: Fasting

Fasting is something nearly everyone can do. Even those not used to fasting or those with rapid metabolisms can fast. It can be a powerful tool for us. It is probably the quickest way to humble ourselves (see Psalm 35:13) and one of the greatest ways to express our love.

I used to hate fasting. I still don't enjoy it, but I don't hate it anymore. I used to fast weekly and it became a burden. To SURVIVE A FAST, I used to demonize burgers, steaks, and pizza in my mind, seeing them as evil temptations trying to lure me into their trap. Like warding off evil spirits, I would strive to avoid that which I craved.

One day the Lord spoke internally to me about this and it came as a simple question: "Would you prefer Me over food?" Interesting, I thought. That is a different perspective. It was then that I began to see that I had been saying "no" to food, "no" to enjoyment, and "no" to the evils of eating. The Lord, on the other hand wasn't hinting that food was bad; He simply asked if I would prefer to spend my taste buds on Him rather than food for a time. I could do this.

Now, rather than demonizing food, I can say burgers are juicy and inviting, prime rib is mouthwatering and flavorful, and pizza is God's gift to mankind, but I choose to set these wonderful things aside for a time to instead taste of Him and see that He is even better.

With this approach, I prefer the Lord rather than suffering out of obligation. I don't get weird; I don't turn into a resentful faster or Christian who turns mean during fasting. Instead, I'm simply choosing God over food, not hating my existence.

This is why Jesus said:

"But you, when you fast, anoint your head and wash your face

so that your fasting will not be noticed by men, but by your Father who is in secret; and your Father who sees what is done in secret will reward you" (Matthew 6:17-18).

Launch Point: Faith in Action

Disclaimer: For all of the "Faith in Action" suggestions, please make sure that you only do what is physically safe for you to attempt and, if possible, plan to have a buddy with you. Although it is necessary to live by faith, it is also important to use wisdom. Do not place yourself in any situation that makes you uncomfortable or concerned for your physical safety.

I once attempted to learn a foreign language while living in Asia by hiring a Harvard educated language instructor. She was an older woman who was very qualified to teach her native tongue. After several weeks of trying to teach me, she quit. She said that I would never learn the language she was trying to teach me because I would never practice it. She was right. I wanted to speak fluently without the "baby steps" necessary to get there. I was too embarrassed to speak with mistakes. I wanted it to come quickly, poetically, and without effort, perfectly annunciated. Sadly, I never learned that language.

In similar fashion, I've come to realize that we will not raise the dead, see people healed, live supernaturally, or do any **"greater works" (see John 14:12)** until we begin to practice, step out, and exercise the legs and arms of our spirit man. Just as muscles begin to atrophy without use, OUR SPIRIT MAN REQUIRES EXERCISE on the treadmill of faith in order to grow in strength and power.

The actions of faith within this guide may seem random or not "led" by the Holy Spirit. I've found that stepping out with a heart of love for people will result in God using us to impact lives in powerful ways.

The most exciting moments in my life have come as I stepped out when I didn't "feel" like it, letting God move through me by loving people through kind words, encouraging hope, or praying for them.

Jesus mentioned to His own brothers that their time is **"always opportune" (see John 7:6)** to display the works of Christ. I believe that every day presents opportunities for us to display the love and power of Christ. Our time is always.

Launch Point: Praying in the Spirit

Being filled with the Spirit and praying in the Spirit are different experiences. Being filled with the Spirit is described previously (Launch Point: Filled with the Spirit, pages 157-158). Praying in the Spirit is when we engage our spirits with heaven and the INDWELLING HOLY SPIRIT, praying that which we may not understand with our minds. This type of prayer can be as varied and unique as the Holy Spirit Himself is unique. Sometimes the prayers may be warlike, or soft and worshipful, or they may even sound Asian or Germanic. Sometimes the prayers turn into the song of heaven and sounds we have never heard before. We may pray in the Spirit in numerous ways. We have an untethered God without limitation. As we enter His realm, we will begin praying in wonderful ways that express things beyond our understanding.

> **"But you, beloved, building yourselves up on your most holy faith, praying in the Holy Spirit,**

"keep yourselves in the love of God, waiting anxiously for the mercy of our Lord Jesus Christ to eternal life" (Jude 20-21).

Throughout eternity, we will pray and this is our practice ground, this life is our entry point into the ways of God.

Launch Point: Exercise

In our generally sedentary society, it is important to exercise regularly in order to maintain the level of health that will enable us to live long enough to fulfill our purposes. This should also include eating healthy food that provides our bodies what it needs to function well and think clearly.

We are not just a spirit or a mind in a body. Our body is going to be with us for a very long time—eternally. Jesus still has the body He had when He walked the earth two thousand years ago. It's been changed, but it still is a part of who He is now in heaven. His nail-pierced hands are still with Him and will always be.

If we could see ourselves as not just internally eternal beings, but wholly eternal beings, then taking care of our physical bodies is also important because GOD FORMED OUR BODIES (see Psalm 149), made us unique, and loves all that He has made us to be. We are wholly His. The devil doesn't own our bodies. We are all parts of His and our bodies are a house for the Holy Spirit (see I Corinthians 6), worthy of attention, maintenance, and care so that our purposes are not cut short due to neglect.

If we are one hundred pounds overweight, in addition to our heart not being healthy, what if God asked us to go build a church on the mission field or to work in a job requiring physical movement? It would be very difficult to do so. Making a plan to take care of our bodies will help eliminate our excuses for not being able to do and go wherever He sends us.

There are numerous non-gimmicky ways to lose weight and maintain sound health. Your local gym or YMCA will have helpful advice also.

Launch Point: Serving

Jesus said that He didn't come to be served, but TO SERVE OTHERS (see Matthew 20:28). He also said that the greatest among us are the servants of all (see Matthew 23:11). These are strong statements that directly confront the "man of God" untouchable mentality that has pervaded certain aspects of the church. Jesus not only made these statements, He also girded Himself with a towel and began washing the feet of His friends who would all abandon Him hours later. Jesus didn't serve the deserving, He served those He loved. He demonstrated to us yet another aspect of ministry, humbling ourselves and meeting the needs of others at the very moment when our own needs appear to be more important.

The greater we grow in knowledge, abilities, skills, and anointing, should also correspond with greater humility in service. When Billy Graham was voted one of the most respected people in our country, he went to personally see one of the most despised people in our country, Jim Bakker, while he was in prison and ministered to him. That is serving. Ministry is not about knowing more than those we lead, but leveraging our knowledge with the power of love to serve those we lead.

Serving others also does something inside of us. It takes our minds off our problems, needs, and issues, and gets us engaged with becoming an answer for someone else's problems. When this occurs, our perspective tends to be transformed and our issues diminished.

Launch Point: Believe

Your appellation is a "BELIEVER," a Christian. Being called a "believer" and actually believing on a daily basis are two different things. Believing isn't just a title or grouping, it is the activity that saves us, heals us, and provides the pathway for us to live eternally with God. Believing is one of our primary jobs and the only way that we will see the kingdom of God manifested through us. Without believing, we receive nothing other than double mindedness.

Jesus abolished toil and was the fulfillment of the law of works, so we don't have to strive and toil any longer trying to please God. We have a new job description and a new occupation in the New Covenant—the full-time occupation of believing.

Jesus said it like this: **"This is the work of God, that you believe in Him whom He has sent" (see John 6:29).**

The work of believing indicates that there will be a good amount of the opposite to work through, and there is. Unbelief, the structure of intellectualism, and the missiles of doubt fired at us, provide an interesting work environment. A work environment is similar to a battlefield, with the enemy shooting thousands of missiles of doubt and poison-tipped arrows in the form of questions our way, attempting to kill and steal our attention and life.

Aware of this, we choose to "work" by believing anyway, keeping our eyes and hearts fixed entirely on our Champion, on His Words, and mindful of His victory in which He already defeated the missile thrower. We choose to cast down all vain imaginations, shrug off all voices of doubt and depression, choosing to live up to our title—believers who are actively at work believing.

Launch Point: Break a Cycle

Whether it's pornography, criticism, lust, gossip, or addictions of any kind, Jesus has provided the way for us to be entirely free. He came to SET EVERY CAPTIVE free and give us abundant life in exchange for our sins and bondages.

Oftentimes, it is the thief that we didn't know was there that steals from us the most. For many, criticism is that thief. Both Jesus and Paul (see Matthew 7:1 and Romans 2:1) describe how criticism and judging others will cause us to do the very thing we have criticized. Criticism is like a boomerang that we launch into the air unaware of its returning quality. It will come back around and knock us in the forehead later.

We can break the cycle of addiction and criticism by simply recognizing and taking ownership for what we have done, shove it into the light (see I John 1:7-9), and ask forgiveness. Then, we break the cycle of our bondage by doing the opposite—releasing blessing and encouragement rather than judgment, and honoring rather than criticizing. Breaking this cycle will bring healing to our marriages, homes, and jobs.

"So if the Son makes you free, you will be free indeed" (see John 8:36).

Launch Point: Agreement

"Do two men walk together unless they have made an appointment?" (Amos 3:3)

The ENEMY WAS DEFEATED BY JESUS two thousand years ago. What remains of him is the power to deceive. His deceptions and lies are nothing more than his efforts to get us into agreements with what he says. Our agreement with him regarding anything he says gives him power as he leverages our faith to believe in his lies. Since Jesus took back the keys from the devil and has given us authority, the devil's power must come through us "walking" with him in his lies.

His desire is to usurp our authority to subdue the earth, using it to bring darkness on the earth.

This is why we want to be proclaimers of truth, believers of God's Words about us, and not in agreement with death.

By intentionally breaking agreement with any and all lies that the enemy has placed in our minds throughout our lives, we break his power over and through us.

Launch Point: Proclamation

The Lord "SPOKE," and things that did not previously exist suddenly took form, coming into being. The tool the Creator used to form the heavens and the earth were *words* such as "Let." By speaking out loud into nothingness, He "allowed" planets to form and the elements of dirt to unite. When God made mankind, He did it a bit differently. Using the dirt He had "let" happen, He bent down and used His own hands to form mankind to look like Himself. With the first complete human lifeless in His arms, He then took the same air that had previously spoken into nothingness and "breathed" His air between the lips and into the lungs of Adam, bringing him to life. Adam then not only looked like Him, but he had been touched by Him and breathed into by Him. You and I still carry that breath of God, and even greater, we have become the "mobile" homes of God (see I Corinthians 6) with Him inside.

Those created by Him with His breath inside are able to do what Jesus did and greater (see John 14:12).

Our words have creative power. Our words, like our Father and His Son's, have power to both produce and remove, to curse or to bless, to build up or to destroy. What we say has "allowing" power. This is why the enemy expends so much energy attempting to coerce us and voice our agreement with his lies, "allowing" his plans to take place instead of God's.

Therefore, one of the powerful weapons in our arsenal is the use of our words— particularly our words that align with the kingdom, the word, and truth. Our verbal proclamation of what is true, what is real, what has been done, what will be done, what should be done, and what is full of hope begins the creative process in the atmosphere.

Your proclamation over yourself and others "allows" or releases the elements of good or evil to begin moving. I've personally found that proclaiming that which is true, even if I don't "feel it," pushes me to faith. Faith combined with words moves mountains and changes the course of history. We get to be proclaimers of truth, declarers of God's purposes.

Launch Point: Celebration

God mandated times of CELEBRATION for Israel throughout the Old Covenant. There were weeklong feasts, festivities, and lots of eating and enjoyment. There were also celebrations for walls being completed, enemies vanquished, and the ark returning to Israel. In the New Covenant, we find that the first miracle of Jesus takes place at a wedding celebration, where He turned somewhere between 120 to 180 gallons of water into well-aged wine. When Jesus told the story about the prodigal son, He shared how the father threw a celebration for his returning son. At the conclusion of the Scriptures, we see the grand finale celebration ushering in a new era with the bride and the Son.

Celebration is more common in the Bible than mourning and mandated more than fasting. Heaven will be an enormous celebration and is a kingdom dynamic where we can be creative and learn to be lavish.

The spirit of religion strangles celebration of every kind, turning joy into work and rejoicing into duty.

the Extraordinary Journey

Miscellaneous "X" Stuff

I've highlighted the "X" in "eXtraordinary" for several reasons. The "X" is the shape of the 22nd letter in the original Hebrew alphabet, meaning "simple faith." "X" also refers to the first letter of the Greek name for Christ or Christos, signifying the person of Jesus. Slightly tilted, the Hebrew "X" is also the shape of the cross, and to me symbolizes the extraordinary prophetic symbol of the New Covenant, freedom, and life we can have in Christos, or Christ, the Anointed One. In addition, both men and women have "X" chromosomes, speaking of the DNA of Christ in us. For fun, the Lord gave women double "X" chromosomes—twice as much Christ, which may have finally answered the question of why there are typically twice as many women in the church as men.

I also wanted to use the "X" in a positive way, turning the tables on the "X-Rated" connotation that the enemy has created.

MorningStar University
SCHOOL OF MINISTRY　SCHOOL OF BUSINESS　SCHOOL OF WORSHIP ARTS

RELEASING A SUPERNATURAL ARMY TO TRANSFORM THE WORLD

BUILD STRONG BIBLICAL FOUNDATIONS AND A CHRISTIAN WORLDVIEW

GAIN PRACTICAL AND SUPERNATURAL TOOLS FOR SUCCESS

ENGAGE IN "SPECIAL FORCES" MISSION OPPORTUNITIES

INTERN WITH INTERNATIONAL MINISTRY, EDUCATION, AND BUSINESS LEADERS

1, 2, AND 3 YEAR PROGRAMS AVAILABLE
* ASSOCIATE DEGREES AVAILABLE

NOW ACCEPTING APPLICATIONS

FIND YOUR DESTINY　　IMPACT HISTORY　　CHANGE THE WORLD

FOR MORE INFORMATION

CALL: 803-802-5544, EXTENSION 238
VISIT: WWW.MORNINGSTARMINISTRIES.ORG
EMAIL: MSUOffice@MorningStarMinistries.org

Every 15 seconds a person dies from water-related diseases

zao water is actively engaged in transforming villages in the developing world from places of hopelessness and disease to places that thrive with life. By providing clean natural water, supernatural living water, and hygiene training, our mission is to bring the abundant life of Jesus to the nations.

BECOME A PART OF THE ZaO MISSION!

- *Sponsor a well or a spring*
- *Partner with ZaO to hydrate humanity*

SIGN UP AT:
www.hydratinghumanity.com

For as little as $5 a month, you can make a difference. $5 = clean water for five people FOR ONE YEAR.

zao
hydrating humanity

www.hydratinghumanity.com
www.zaowater.com 888.zao.water
office@zaowater.com